FINANCIAL
FITNESS
FOR
NEW FAMILIES

FINANCIAL
FITNESS
FOR
NEW FAMILIES

Elizabeth S. Lewin, CFP

Facts On File
New York • Oxford • Sydney

Financial Fitness for New Families

Copyright © 1989 by Elizabeth S. Lewin

All rights reserved. No part of this book may be reproduced or utilized in any form or by any means, electronic or mechanical, including photocopying, recording, or by any information storage and retrieval systems, without permission in writing from the publisher. For information contact:

Facts On File, Inc.
460 Park Avenue South
New York NY 10016
USA

Facts On File, Limited
Collins Street
Oxford OX4 1XJ
United Kingdom

Facts On File Pty Ltd
Talavera & Khartoum Rds
North Ryde NSW 2113
Australia

Library of Congress Cataloging-in-Publication Data

Lewin, Elizabeth
    Financial fitness for new families/Elizabeth S. Lewin.
       p. cm.
    ISBN 0-8160-1980-0
    1. Finance, Personal. I. Title
HG179.L474 1989
332.024—dc20   89-17110

British and Australian CIP data available on request from Facts On File.

ISBN 0-8160-1980-0

Facts On File books are available at special discounts when purchased in bulk quantities for businesses, associations, institutions or sales promotion. Please contact the Special Sales Department of our New York office at 212/683–2244 (dial 800/322–8755 except in NY, AK or HI).

Composition by Facts On File, Inc.
Manufactured by Viking Press Inc.
Printed in the United States of America

10 9 8 7 6 5 4 3 2 1

This book is printed on acid–free paper.

To my daughter and son-in-law, Valerie and James; my son, Eric and his wife, Jeanne; and to the other couples who shared their goals, dreams and finances with me.

ACKNOWLEDGMENTS

My special appreciation to Bernard Ryan, Jr., whose help made all this possible, and to Sue L. Hudson, whose insights into the psychological aspects of the subject were invaluable.

I also wish to thank Myron I. Dworken, CPA, Laventhol & Horvath; and Elena Keaveney, Smith, Barney, Harris, Upham & Co.

CONTENTS

WHY I WROTE THIS BOOK

1

This book is for new couples and new parents. It is for any two people who have recently begun to operate a single household with probably—at least for the time being—two incomes. And it is for those who have been together for some time and now have the additional financial responsibility for children. Its purpose is to help you attain Personal Financial Fitness together.

I wrote this book because I believe that newlyweds and new parents have special needs and problems, and countless unanswered questions about their personal finances. The newlywed couple may be wondering how to restructure their separate accounts into a joint financial future. The couple with a newborn needs to face a range of costs—most of them substantial—that includes child care, food, and medicine that keeps going up, additional insurance to cover both life and disability, and, off on the horizon, college education. The aim of this book is to help you find practical, workable answers to such questions.

I also wrote this book because I am convinced that your generation does not want to be deprived of the knowledge of how to manage money as my generation was deprived—and as so many generations before us were deprived.

Why doesn't anybody tell children about money? Why don't parents teach money management? Why don't schools? Why do we deprive our children of the knowledge of money, yet ask them to assume adult responsibility for it?

Most parents send their offspring out into the world totally unprepared to handle their personal finances. Somehow they—the parents—think they shouldn't burden their children with "financial problems." They think children will feel secure if they don't have to "worry" about money. In most households, good practical talk about money is heard about as often as good practical talk about sex—almost never. Thus, most young people have to learn about money management by trial and error—like learning about sex. On the other hand, while today sex has become an open topic of conversation between increasing numbers of parents and children, money still is not openly discussed.

Why don't parents and children talk about money?

People shun frank and open discussions about money for many reasons. Some parents don't talk about it just because their parents didn't. Some worry that their children will find out they don't make as much as their neighbors or the parents of peers in school. (Only rarely, however, do parents or children who are keeping up with the Joneses really have an accurate idea of the Joneses' income; when you're keeping up with the Joneses, it could be the Joneses who are keeping up with *you*.) Some parents fight about money so frequently it frightens their children and they become convinced it is a subject to shy away from.

Why couples fight over money

It's generally accepted that money is the most common cause of disagreements (read, "fights") between couples. But often it isn't money itself that's the problem. Frequently a fight over money is a manifestation of some other problem. In the traditional family situation, the husband's value was based on what he earned. The wife, who was not a breadwinner but a homemaker (read, "housewife" in the more familiar stereotype), sought some recognition of her own. She felt entitled to something, wanted to participate somehow or share in the process of managing the household. So—almost as you've seen it in TV sit-coms—she might spend at the wrong moment in the budget schedule, or more than the budget allowed, as a way of showing her entitlement. And a battle royal would ensue. Very likely she would at some point use the words, "I'm entitled to buy…"

Marriage is a financial partnership. Chances are you have received no real training in managing money from your parents (almost certainly you've had none from your schools), and you may find that any strong discussion of money follows lines of emotion rather than reason. It's really very hard to have a financial discussion that doesn't become emotional. Remember, a reasonable discussion never becomes a fight. An emotional discussion usually does become a fight, if not a pitched battle. One of my main purposes in writing this book is to help you avoid not only the battles but the lesser fights, too.

What is money?

Good question. Compound answer: Money is a symbol that has many emotional and psychological meanings. It is…

- *Success.* Money is the standard measure.
- *Security.* If only you can get enough money, you'll have no problems. Nice thought. Things aren't all that simple, however.
- *Power.* Money can enable you to buy, manipulate, control—not only things but people. Sometimes.
- *Love.* Money provides a way to show affection. It's a measure of caring. It's birthday and Christmas checks from Gramps and Grannie.
- *Anger.* Sometimes even hate. Money withheld is punishment, an inducement toward changed behavior.
- *Freedom.* Money gives independence from the control of another.

A medium of exchange

Forget all the symbolic meanings of money. Look at it for what it really is: *a medium of exchange for the goods and services we need and desire.* Think of it as a useful tool. Like a power mower, maybe. You can learn how to run it to trim and control your ever-growing environment, when to let it sit idle, how to keep it from getting out of control. But remember: If you don't learn how to handle it, it can cut off your toes.

The key word is *awareness.* You need to be aware of why you handle money the way you do, and of what changes in behavior you may need to make to put you in control of your money—so that you don't find it in control of you.

By managing your money soundly, you will cut down on anxiety and frustration. You will find yourself living within your income, taking care of your own financial needs, reaching your financial goals.

This book shows you practical ways of getting the most value out of money as a medium of exchange, to help give you the kind of life you want. I'll try not to preach. I've concentrated on demonstrating how the money you make can be managed to provide the home and lifestyle, the travel and other leisure–time activities, child care, the education of your children, the protection against possible setbacks—all the things you are likely to desire and need throughout your life.

Money and age bracket

Let's begin by thinking about various aspects of money—or of money-handling—and how they relate to various periods of a lifetime. Think of it this way: What you do with money is earn it, spend it, borrow it, preserve it, protect it, save it and invest it.

Ideally, you do all of this *all through your life*. But at different stages you do more of one thing than another. At some stages you may be earning less money than you have available for spending, and so you borrow, sensibly. At other stages you should be able to save and invest more than you can at some earlier stages. Always you should be careful to preserve and protect your money.

A good way to think about it is to anticipate six periods of living. But don't become obsessed with the idea that they are absolute. Don't expect some visible road sign to come along to tell you when you move from one into another. Here they are, with some clues as to how your emphasis on earning, spending, borrowing, preserving, protecting, saving and investing your money can be expected to change during each period.

Age 18 to 24

This is when your *earning* will be at its lowest, at least until you retire. It's when you're training for your career, maybe getting a household established, discovering the fun (and the headaches!) of being financially independent of your parents, and setting up your budget and financial systems.

This is always a time when it's easy to make some common mistakes about money-handling—such as over-committing your income, not making both short- and long-term financial plans and goals, not using the help of professional experts, or over-emphasizing your current needs without anticipating changes in your life cycle that are sure to come.

Most desirable in this period: enough income to supply your basic wants and needs, a careful analysis of your financial needs and an ability to live within your income. This is the time to develop your knowledge and skills as a consumer so you can make the best use of your spending, and also to develop a balanced plan for spending, borrowing and saving in the years ahead.

Additional responsibilities: If you are married, and already have one or more children, you should be saving toward owning your own home and buying enough life insurance to cover you and your spouse or whoever the major earners in the household may be. You and your spouse should have made separate wills, making sure that they have included plans for your children if both of you should die. And at a very young age, your children should be learning how to handle money.

If you are married but do not have children, you should nevertheless each have wills. Plans should be established toward owning a home, and you should have a careful agreement on how you divide your financial obligations.

If you are a single parent, have you developed long-term goals for improving your economic position? Do you have a credit rating in your own name? What about arrangements for your children to be taken care of if you should die?

Age 25 to 34

This is the period when *spending* is likely to creep up on earning and when *borrowing* can be expected to keep pace with spending. Everything is increasing, stretching, demanding: The cost of having children and bringing them up hits hard. Probably you have to expand your housing and meet an increased need for credit. Your career goals are sure to be rising, with job changes needed to meet them. More insurance is in order, plus a plan for covering the education of your children. If you haven't made wills, you'd better get at it. And everyone in the family should be learning about money and honing their financial skills.

Mistakes are easy to make. Over-commitment of income is a common one. No emergency fund, not enough savings, no plans for education, insufficient insurance, no realistic personal or family goals—these are just a few common errors. One of the biggest is the failure to get all members of the family, especially the children, involved in financial matters.

Additional responsibilities: If you are married and have children, have you made plans for their education? Are you covering your increasing financial risks, planning for financing the expanded housing you are sure to need? If you do not have children but you and your spouse are both working, how about analyzing methods for reducing your income taxes, and stepping up your savings and investments for your own future security?

Single parent? How are you planning to increase your income, both now and years from now? Are your children developing their financial skills?

Age 35 to 44

Earning is building, perhaps rapidly, in this period. So is spending. In fact, spending may surpass earnings, so that shrewd borrowing is called for. *Protecting* thus becomes a key factor: You need insurance that is more than adequate to protect the family's major earner. For yourselves, more career training may be in order. For your children, the education fund must build strongly now. And a new word is on the horizon: retirement.

Mistakes? Errors? These are easy to make. Many families overuse credit. They don't think of planning to pay for major replacements of automobiles and appliances. They push retirement out of their thoughts. They sit in a job situation that is comfortable when they should increase the family's primary income or look for other sources of income. They let themselves get stymied by their increasing financial needs—and the complexity of those needs. And they don't set up education funds that will be imperative for their children.

Additional responsibilities: If you are married and have no children, it is vital that you both take advantage of your incomes to maximize your investments and savings. If you have parents or others for whom you may be responsible, this is the time to plan their financial future. If you are a single parent, you must make plans for handling the increasing cost of bringing up your children.

Age 45 to 54

Earnings are starting to peak. The children are in—or maybe even getting through—college. If children are in college, you have extraordinary expenses and are possibly borrowing to meet them. If there are no longer any tuition bills, spending may drop (at last!) below earnings, so that borrowing can slacken off. That means saving and investing can grow, too. Protection is still important. Retirement plans should now be discussed regularly, put on paper, worked out. And here comes

another new term: estate plan. Family members should talk about it and figure out what will be needed. Another concern at this age: parents or older dependents—and their future financial needs.

Where can you go wrong? Not adjusting to changing lifestyles. Not providing funds for retirement, or not enough funds. Not understanding and being realistic about both government and private pension plans. Not managing your increased income. Not using professional expert skills that are available.

Additional responsibilities: Now your children are probably leaving home. Does that make a difference in housing costs? Do you need as big a house as you've gotten used to? Is your will up to date? What other legal papers should you review and update?

Age 55 to 64

Earnings really are at their peak now. If your children are on their own, spending is well down, with borrowing at a minimum. This is the time to consolidate your financial assets and provide for future security, looking at tax–shelter programs, asset management, investment opportunities—all those things that seemed like mere pipe dreams 20 years ago. You may want to think about how you will transfer property—your home or other assets. You may want to look into part–time or volunteer work when you do retire. You may find yourself contemplating a move to another climate or an area where the cost of living is lower.

What mistakes can you make, despite the figurative (if not real) gray hairs you will now have? Not enough supplemental retirement funds, beyond your company's pension and Social Security income. Not adjusting to changes in your income. Not readjusting your insurance coverage. Your wills and estate plan may be out of date and your knowledge of the resources right in your own community may be lacking.

Additional responsibilities: If you do not have children, have you set up a plan for what would happen if you and your spouse both died at the same time?

Over 65

Preserving your money—that's the name of the game at this point. As life expectancy has increased, so has the importance of adjusting your lifestyle and living conditions in relation to your income from pensions, savings and investments, as well as to your health.

Now it is important to get help: You need reliable advice on managing personal and economic matters. What are your estate plans at this point, and—let's face it—have you drafted a letter of last instructions?

The common mistakes that many people over 65 make include not doing some of the above, as well as not considering alternative lifestyles in alternative settings, not taking advantage of the resources of their communities, not adjusting spending to their economic situations, not financing their increased leisure activities.

Additional responsibilities: Now it is important to discuss with your children your particular wishes for your future living arrangements, about what is to be done if you cannot take care of yourself, about whether they will need to supplement your income. If you do not have children, you must face such questions as whether your spouse will be taken care of—financially and otherwise—if you die first, what living adjustment each of you will make in case of the partner's illness or death, and what the options are among hospitals, nursing homes and retirement homes.

That's it, the broad, overall things–to–think–about reasons why I wrote this book. I've tried to summarize it all, in a relatively simple fashion, one decade at a time, to give you a general background for the detailed chapters that follow.

INTRODUCING THREE VERY SPECIAL COUPLES...

...the Nicholses, the McQuarters, and the Bucks. Each is a typical couple who will turn up here and there throughout these pages to illustrate how to apply some of the principles and advice in this book to your own situation.

Jeanne and Eric Nichols

Eric and Jeanne Nichols have been married for a little over a year. They met at an intensive baking course at one of the country's most prestigious culinary schools. They had both been working in the food and restaurant field for several years before they met.

Jeanne worked in a gourmet store while she attended her local community college. After gradua-

tion, she went to work for a restaurant chain and soon became an assistant manager. At the same time, she took many professional cooking classes. The restaurant asked her to relocate and manage a new restaurant. "By that time," she says, "I had had it with the crazy hours. I really had no desire to move." Instead, she applied for the intensive baking course and was accepted. After graduation, she landed a job with a corporate catering company.

Jeanne's job? Managing a take–out and catering deli in a corporate park. "We provide the morning muffins and all sorts of food for lunch. A customer can eat in or take the food back to the office. We also cater a lot of meetings and office parties. I get in early in the morning to bake the muffins. And I've got to tell you—in the food business, having a Monday–to–Friday job is just great."

Eric started baking while he was in a work–study program in high school. He went on with it while he went to college. After a couple of years, he decided to relocate, so he could see another part of the country. Not only did he get a job in a bakery and then become pastry chef for a new restaurant—the scrumptious desserts he turned out also brought him rave reviews. When the chef he worked with moved to a country club, Eric went along. "The hours were insane—I worked a split shift, going to work in the morning and staying through lunch, then going back at 5:00 in the afternoon and working until we closed the kitchen. I did that until I went into the baking class."

Now Eric also works for a delicatessen and has regular hours. He and Jeanne both get Sundays off—a rarity in the food business. In fact, as they admit, the hours and the demands in the food business are crazy. They each understand what the other is going through, and they both realize they will probably never have exactly the same hours.

Currently Jeanne is earning $30,000 and Eric is bringing in $29,000. "Our first goal is to buy a house," says Eric. "The suburb we live in is expensive like all large eastern cities. We pay a fortune in rent." Neither of them gets any fringe benefits from his or her employer.

The Nicholses were able to invest a good part of the money they received as wedding gifts. They had both lived independently, so they simply had to merge their possessions. They had no need, as do many newlyweds, for kitchen equipment. And they are careful to keep on saving each month, because they know they will need a hefty sum for the down payment on a home. They did, however, come into the marriage with some long–term debt—each had a car and student loans to pay off.

Valerie and James McQuarter

Married for six years, Valerie and James are musicians. They live in Texas, a state they moved to after they figured out that, in their profession, they could probably make a better living there than anywhere else. One month they feel rich, the next poor. "Our income goes up and down like a yo–yo," says Valerie. "We've really had to work out a tight budget and stick to it."

When Valerie and James were first married, she owned a beat–up car that was not long for this world. It died soon after they moved to Texas, and they used wedding–gift money for the down payment on a new car. The bank refused to lend them the balance without a co–signer because their income was not "steady."

A few years after they were married, Valerie received an inheritance. They used it for the down payment on a house. "We bought the house because the property was what we were looking for," says James. "We were able to work out the financing with the seller. The house was in very sad shape. So, I went to work for a builder for several months, putting up tract homes, and learned everything I could so I could rebuild our home. We do it one step at a time—meaning when we have the money. This house is a great investment. It can only go up in value."

Their son, Taylor, is now a "terrible two." Valerie and James have to carry their own medical insurance, and it covered very little of the expenses of Taylor's birth. "We are savers…we saved for Taylor's birth and we save for the materials we need to remodel the house." They realize that careful budgeting has saved them from the financial pitfalls that are often the undoing of people with unsteady incomes. "We go from month to month never knowing exactly what our income will be. It can be nerve–wracking, but neither one of us would do anything else," says Valerie.

Karen and Pat Buck

Karen and Pat Buck are both in their mid 30s. They have two children—Landon, who is five, and Megan, who is two.

When they were married eight years ago, Pat had just earned his MBA and had accepted a job as salesman for a national card company. Now he has worked his way up to sales manager for one of the company's districts, with his offices in the corporate headquarters. Moving up in his career in sales has meant moving geographically several times to various areas of the country. Karen, at the same time, has been a public relations and advertising professional since she graduated from college.

For Karen and Pat, married life began in a cramped one–bedroom apartment. Then they were able to buy a condominium, and fairly soon after trade it up to a house. "Fortunately, we bought our first house in an area that wasn't too expensive," says Pat. "When we had to move, we made a good gain. So we used that to buy a more expensive house with the next move. We've been lucky with real estate. We've had good gains on the houses we've sold so each gain is rolled over into another more expensive house. And, the company has picked up all the closing costs and moving expenses each time."

But each move did involve dipping into savings for new furniture, draperies and other household items. The Bucks have been in their present home nearly two years and expect that they will stay located at the corporate headquarters for a while.

Landon was born five years ago. "Living expenses were very reasonable where we lived then," says Karen, "so I was able to take a year off from work. The house payments weren't out of sight and we had done a lot of saving during the four years before Landon was born. After a year came another promotion for Pat, and we had to move. Now, the house payments and other expenses skyrocketed. Our savings started to dwindle. So I went back to work on a part–time basis. Then, Megan was born—just before this last move. We couldn't find housing we could afford anywhere near corporate headquarters. The prices of houses in the area? A real shocker! We had to settle in a town about 30 miles from Pat's work. He commutes—bumper–to–bumper—when he isn't traveling. We had sold a house worth $125,000. Well, anything even comparable costs double that around here. And everything else seems to be twice as expensive, too! We really couldn't afford to buy the house, yet it was exactly what we wanted. So that meant back to work full time for me, just to make ends meet. And to save for what we'll need as the kids get older."

Pat's company provides excellent benefits—medical and dental, life and disability insurance, pension and pre–tax savings plans. Pat says, "I have socked away money in the savings plan from the day I started working for the company. It's such a painless way to save. And, with company contributions, I've built up quite a nest egg. If it weren't for that, I probably wouldn't be saving anything. I would love it if Karen could stay home with the children, but that is just not economically possible."

WHY MANAGE MONEY? 2

We fall in love. We marry, we live together, we have two incomes coming in and often we do not communicate about our money. We go from paycheck to paycheck spending on all sorts of consumer goods, saving for a vacation for the next year—but with no long–term plans.

Why manage money? Why set financial goals?

Because it will cut down on anxiety and frustration. Because it puts you both in charge. Because you can actually make it fun to handle money. Because, among other things, *marriage is a financial partnership*.

Let me take you back to about the time you were born. In the early to mid–1960s, the silver lining looked permanent. We came out of the 1950s living fairly high on the hog. The typical middle–class American family had a suburban home with a two-car garage and probably two cars in it. Incomes rose steadily. Inflation had not yet reared its head. Spendable income was abundant, and there was plenty to spend it on.

By the mid-1970s, inflation hit and the bubble burst. The energy crisis shot gasoline prices from 30 cents a gallon to over a dollar, then higher. Prices escalated faster than personal incomes. Interest rates soared. Parents went around the house screaming: "Turn off the lights." "Why do you have to use that hair drier twice in one day?" "What do you mean, you've got to make another trip downtown?"

By the 1980s many young people were making three times as much as their parents had ever dreamed of making, yet were not living as well as their parents had once lived. But they had a range of financial options that had not been available to their parents.

- New financial products: half a dozen types of savings accounts at every savings bank and the "money market" or "liquid assets" funds that compete with savings bank accounts.
- Variable–rate mortgage loans: Home buyers could now take their chances on inflation coming down in three years, and the interest rate dropping with it. (Or, both can rise.)
- Revolving charge accounts: "cash reserve" banking, which allows you to overdraw your checking account with every check you write, and

catch up with every deposit—so long as you keep making more deposits and paying the finance charges. And VISA and MasterCard invite you to keep charging, paying up, charging again.

- Deregulation of fixed–term savings certificates: banks paying whatever interest rates they choose on fixed–term accounts running more than 31 days. With some certificates investors may set their own maturity dates; penalties on early withdrawals have been relaxed.

This changing economy and the new financial options are important for people of all ages. For those of you who have recently married, "we" and "us" are now replacing the "me" and "I." You are now a team and you are putting together a financial partnership. The birth of a child adds new financial responsibilities and obligations. If you don't recognize and discuss the need to manage money, you could buy trouble.

A million choices

You have immediate choices and long–term choices to make. Should you buy furniture? A car? Rent an apartment? Buy a condominium? A house? Start a family? Spend on vacations and travel during your first two or three years of marriage and then have children? Get more education so you can qualify for better jobs? Take on a second job, to add income? Return to work after the birth of a child?

The result of all these possibilities is bewilderment that your parents may never have had to cope with at the same age.

Don't think you won't make mistakes. And don't be afraid to make some. Everybody does, at one time or another. I hope that, as marital financial partners living together, you have already seen the need to communicate about money. Good financial habits—*mutually agreeable* financial habits—have to grow out of communication. If they start to grow early in your marriage, you will find it a lot easier than if you wait until some crisis forces you into trying to set up some good financial habits.

The key thing to communicate is goals.

Everybody needs financial goals

True. Everybody needs financial goals. But you are the only two people who know what your particular goals

are. And only you two—together—can put your goals on paper so you can set up a sensible framework for reaching them. Writing them down on paper will enable you to:

- View money as more than something to have and use here and now. Most people have very little concept of money for the future, for the expensive trip next year or the year after, for the car to replace this car, for the major anniversary. They'll think about that next year—or the year after. But then it will be too late.
- Establish a way of gaining financial security. This means having a steady source of income and seeing that it increases each year to keep up with inflation and with your needs and desires; having money set aside for emergencies small (getting a broken appliance fixed) or large (an unexpected medical expense); having protection in case of disability or death.
- Utilize your income to best advantage. This means planning for your home, vacations, family.
- Accept the reality of your particular situation. This means spending against your plan, rather than against a dream.

In addition to writing them down, you and your spouse must talk freely, openly, at length about your goals. You must communicate your individual financial objectives to each other and reach a good understanding about them.

How do you establish your goals?

The first question is, What's important to us? Your goals reflect two value systems: the attitudes each of you were raised with. They may be almost the same. They may have some variances you didn't even know existed until you started talking about them. So it's important for you to figure out where each of you is "coming from." And where you want to go.

For most people, values are based on what is desirable and worthy. And the value systems of most people are usually fairly inflexible. They are passed down from grandparents and parents. All the more reason for lots of open talk, because values produce attitudes.

Values are tied closely to ego fulfillment. And ego fulfillment is tied closely to money. Money, in turn, is a major measure of success. And success brings the circle around again to ego fulfillment.

The fulfillment of one's ego, and one's involvement in his or her success, may often leave little room for recognition of what's going on with a mate's success—or lack of it. The result is the stuff of which TV situation comedies have been made for many years: wives who don't understand how hard a husband is working ("Another business trip? Another three-day vacation in Chicago?")...husbands who don't appreciate how successfully a wife is managing household finances...spending to "get even" (yes, corny as it sounds, it does happen). And there are husbands who don't understand the ego fulfillment—measured by earnings—that a working wife is getting from a full-time job.

Often, success and ego fulfillment are communicated through material signs. A Mercedes-Benz automobile, Gucci shoes, a Louis Vuitton bag, a Hermes scarf, an Izod Lacoste shirt—these tell the world that the owner belongs to the right group. They are used to demonstrate that one is successful in our society, for one can afford its trappings. Although their owners may not talk about such signs very much, values are expressed by them.

Values also dictate habits. And habits set priorities. Suppose you've been raised with a value system that says home ownership is a must. That may dictate saving $150 a month for a down payment. But maybe your habits conflict with reaching that goal. You decide you cannot save $150 a month. Or you put another goal first—maybe traveling before you start a family, or owning a boat, or buying a sports car. Your habits are then showing you that the home-owning goal is a lower priority than your value system said it was.

Goals have priorities

Put each of your goals into one of the following categories:

- *Short-term goals.* What you need for next year. Paying for some furniture. Planning Christmas shopping. Buying a vacation in advance, so you have the money in hand on the day you set out.
- *Middle-term goals.* Three to five years away. Buying a house. Or off-road vehicle. Raising your children at today's projected costs of $225,000 per

child from age 1 to 22. Children are definitely part of your middle- and long-range goals.
- *Long-term goals.* Education for the children. A second home for weekends. Retirement.

Interest rates and inflation

Since the mid-70s we have been living with inflation. By the end of that decade, we had an annual inflation rate in the double digits. Though it has moderated, we still worry about inflation. What inflation does is erode the value or purchasing power of our money.

Exhibit 1
INFLATION FACTOR

Number of Years Till Goal	Inflation Rate		
	5%	7%	10%
2	1.10	1.13	1.22
3	1.15	1.20	1.34
4	1.22	1.29	1.48
5	1.29	1.41	1.62
6	1.36	1.52	1.78
7	1.43	1.64	1.96
8	1.50	1.75	2.16
9	1.58	1.88	2.38
10	1.65	2.00	2.60

Thus, if your goal is to save $10,000 in 10 years, you would need $16,500 with a 5 percent annual rate of inflation and $20,000 with a 7 percent annual rate of inflation. In other words, it would take $16,500 in 10 years to buy what $10,000 buys today, assuming a 5 percent rate of inflation.

When we talk about saving for a goal, you have to take into consideration the return you will receive on your money. If you put $100 under your mattress, you will still have only $100 next year or in five or 10 years. But if that $100 earns 7 percent interest in a bank account, you will have $107.23 in one year (assuming monthly compounding). Look at the chart below to see how much you have to save each month to reach your specific goal. The idea is to have your money earning more than inflation.

Exhibit 2
MONTHLY INVESTMENT DOLLARS NECESSARY TO REACH GOAL

Years Till Goal	2 Years Est. Rates of Return			4 Years Est. Rates of Return			6 Years Est. Rates of Return			8 Years Est. Rates of Return			10 Years Est. Rates of Return		
Goal Amount	6%	8%	10%	6%	8%	10%	6%	8%	10%	6%	8%	10%	6%	8%	10%
$ 5,000	$ 196	193	189	$ 92	89	85	$ 58	54	51	$ 41	37	34	$ 31	27	24
10,000	393	386	378	185	177	170	116	109	102	81	75	68	61	55	49
20,000	786	771	756	370	355	341	231	217	204	163	149	137	122	109	98
30,000	1,180	1,157	1,134	555	532	511	347	326	306	244	224	205	183	164	146
40,000	1,573	1,542	1,512	739	710	681	463	435	408	326	299	273	244	219	195
50,000	1,966	1,928	1,891	924	877	851	579	543	510	407	374	342	305	273	244
60,000	2,359	2,314	2,269	1,109	1,065	1,022	694	652	612	488	448	410	366	328	293
70,000	2,752	2,699	2,647	1,294	1,242	1,192	810	761	713	570	523	479	427	383	342
80,000	3,146	3,085	3,025	1,479	1,420	1,362	926	869	815	651	598	547	488	437	391
90,000	3,539	3,470	3,403	1,664	1,597	1,533	1,042	978	917	733	672	616	549	492	439

Chart assumes constant rate of return, compounded monthly, calculated for deposits made at the end of the month.
Source: Manufacturers Hanover.

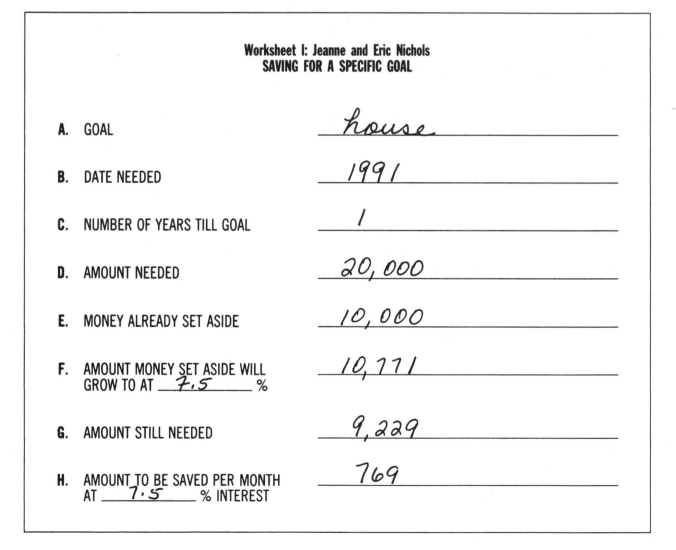

Worksheet I: Jeanne and Eric Nichols
SAVING FOR A SPECIFIC GOAL

A. GOAL — *house*

B. DATE NEEDED — *1991*

C. NUMBER OF YEARS TILL GOAL — *1*

D. AMOUNT NEEDED — *20,000*

E. MONEY ALREADY SET ASIDE — *10,000*

F. AMOUNT MONEY SET ASIDE WILL GROW TO AT __7.5__ % — *10,771*

G. AMOUNT STILL NEEDED — *9,229*

H. AMOUNT TO BE SAVED PER MONTH AT __7.5__ % INTEREST — *769*

The "blind worksheets" on goals.

At this point, why don't each of you list your most important three or four short–term and long–term goals. Do this separately and without comparing notes, then see how close you come to having the same goals. Remember that almost any goal is money–related. For example, if your goal is to play racquetball twice a week, obviously you will have to budget for the court time, and maybe a couple of beers afterward. (Two beers a budget item? Yes, if they are consumed twice a week times 50 or 52 weeks a year.)

The primary objective

Everything in your financial plan is directed to a single goal: the accumulation of capital, or money. This calls not only for good definition of goals but for follow–through on their details. If your top short–term goal is to accumulate a down payment for a home, now is the time to estimate what it will cost, at least in today's dollars. Make the effort to get actual figures on the kind of house you have in mind. Just getting the figures could switch this goal from short–term to middle–term (but not necessarily!). If it does, then be sure to keep tabs on costs so you can update the figures once a year.

This kind of planning and figuring can help you avoid waking up one day to find that you have to borrow to meet a goal because its price kept going up while you weren't looking.

Goals and needs are subject to change. Check them over at least once a year. *Important:* Never feel you must stay locked into a specific goal. Your interests can change. Your needs can change.

Tip: Never use the money set aside for a middle– or long–term goal to pay for something you want now. That's robbing yourselves.

How you benefit from setting goals

Setting goals forces you both to examine your values, to clarify them, to reach understanding and agreement with each other. It forces you to devise ways to use your resources to attain your goals. It gives you control. And it makes you aware that each partner's pattern of behavior for attaining goals—just how you go about reaching them—must be compatible with the other's and both must be consistent with the goals. Otherwise you're headed for conflict and trouble.

In fact, classic confrontations between husbands and wives have occurred because either or both have not let their goals be known. It is imperative that you talk about values and goals with each other. Talk, then talk some more. Set up a system that gives you time to talk when you are both fresh and up to it—not at bedtime, not when you are tired after work, not at dinner with drinks. Make it early in the day, or over brunch on Saturday or Sunday. Give yourselves a reward for good talk about finances—the brunch itself, a place to go, a show to see.

Make money talk fun. It can be. Handling money can be fun and interesting and rewarding, as I hope this book will demonstrate. But you need a system to make it so, to help you deal with any possible conflicting values and find solutions.

Think of such a system as a continuous circular process involving these steps:

1. Identify the problem together. Talk about it openly until you agree on just what it is.
2. Discuss possible solutions. Don't try to settle on any particular solution now—just put every possible (or even remotely possible) solution out on the table.
3. Set it all aside for a while. For at least several hours. Maybe several days or a week.
4. Go back to it and discuss solutions again.
5. Negotiate a resolution together.

THE NICHOLSES ARE DYING TO OWN A HOUSE

Buying a home means more than anything to Jeanne and Eric Nichols. They are currently paying $925 rent each month for a two–bedroom condo. They realize that a mortgage, property taxes and homeowners insurance will add up to more than they are paying in rent, but they will be able to deduct their property taxes and interest on the mortgage from their income taxes. Thus, they will reduce their income taxes and build equity in a home.

They have put aside their wedding–gift money and are saving on a regular basis. To help them focus on their goal of home ownership, Jeanne and Eric put their plan on paper. Worksheet I (p. 12), Saving for A Specific Goal, was the result. For Jeanne and Eric this identified precisely what they needed to do to reach their goal. The figure in line H is the amount that they must save each year, assuming a 7.5 percent interest rate. This figure comes from a book called *Financial Compound Interest and Annuity Tables.*

(Check with your bank, insurance agent or accountant; they have ready access to this particular book.)

Select one of your specific goals. Sit down and fill out the blank copy of Worksheet I. You'll see how it concentrates your attention on what you need to do now to achieve what you want later.

Worksheet I: Yours
SAVING FOR A SPECIFIC GOAL

A. GOAL _____

B. DATE NEEDED _____

C. NUMBER OF YEARS TILL GOAL _____

D. AMOUNT NEEDED _____

E. MONEY ALREADY SET ASIDE _____

F. AMOUNT MONEY SET ASIDE WILL GROW TO AT _____ % _____

G. AMOUNT STILL NEEDED _____

H. AMOUNT TO BE SAVED PER MONTH AT _____ % INTEREST _____

WHO'S GOING TO MANAGE THE MONEY?

3

The next logical question after "Why manage money?" is "Who's going to do it?" And right after that comes "How is it done?" This takes us to *budget*—but I'm getting too far ahead of the story. The three questions are very closely tied together and they obviously overlap in many ways. They are broken into three chapters only for purposes of discussion and clarity.

Some questions to ask one another

Before you can set up a budget, you need to talk out some basic points:

- Who is going to pay for what? What is a workable method of paying bills and putting away savings? Will one of us be in charge of all bill paying? Should we take turns?
- Are we going to try to pay for day-to-day living expenses—food, utilities—out of one salary?
- Will we reserve the other paycheck for savings, investments and extras?
- Should we pool all our income into a single account, paying all bills and setting aside savings from it?

- Or should we maintain separate accounts and each take responsibility for certain expenses?
- Or—a third way—should we set up a joint account for fixed expenses, with separate accounts for other expenses and individual use? This means we must decide how much we will each contribute to the joint account.
- Is one of us better than the other at handling money? This is really the *key* question.

There are no absolute answers to these questions. You have to put your heads together and decide what is best for you *together*, in your situation. And your decision must also fit what is best for each of you *individually*.

Some facts that affect your decisions

In the rare cases where you both earn nearly the same amount, a single pooled account can work out fine. But if one of you earns a good deal more than the other, you may want to keep individual accounts and contribute proportionately to a joint account for paying the day–to–day expenses (more on this in subsequent chapters).

To help keep the chores fairly divided, you might want to split them this way: One of you handles the checkbooks and bill paying, while the other does the record keeping—posts the income and outgo in your budget book, takes care of the filing, and also handles the tax returns. This gives you a sort of mini-auditing system, so you have some checks and balances in your financial partnership. It's not a bad idea from several standpoints: If one of you feels less good at this kind of work than the other, you can learn from your partner. If the check writer and bill payer is straying from systems or goals you agreed on, it will be discovered and you can openly discuss how to fix the problem. And once you have established this system and both know how it all works, you can switch responsibilities if and when you get bored or just feel it's time for a change.

> *Important:* If you set up such a system make sure responsibilities are clearly assigned and kept separate. Don't fall into a situation where both of you are casually writing the checks and keeping the records, because sooner or later one of you will think the other did something—paid some bill, filed some cash register tape—that neither of you did.

Eventually, the best system for handling the money will evolve. From working together you'll see which one of you is better at handling money and actually enjoys it more. You'll find out who has more time for it, or who can take care of it more quickly.

Your job situations can be a factor, too. If one of you is traveling a lot, the other probably should be the money manager. But both of you should be involved. If one spouse is unaware of how the money is managed, a major illness or long business trip can leave the uninvolved spouse out in the cold and at wit's end.

Checks and checkbooks

In most cases, I recommend that each person maintain a separate checking account. Even a non–working spouse should keep an account, if that spouse is handling the food budget, for instance, and may be able to save some of it.

Separate accounts give each of you control over your own income. As long as you know and agree on who is responsible for what, you have no particular need to account to each other for what is in your own accounts. If either of you is able to save a little in your own account, it is yours to do with as you please. If the grocery buyer can save something on the food budget, as mentioned above, there should never be any complaints as long as you are both eating well right through to the last day of the month. *This concept is very important.*

If you are maintaining separate accounts and a joint "household" account, you might want to tie into the new system of telephone bill–paying services that many banks now offer. This can cut down on check writing time and give you an easy way to pay rent, mortgage, utilities, American Express card accounts, department stores—even, in some communities, the garbage collector.

Orderly checkbooks are vital—whether for separate accounts or a joint account. An excellent habit to get into is that of writing the check stub *first*, before you write the check. Be sure to put down what the check is for, not just to whom it is payable, on the stub. This will be important for your budgeting process.

> *Tip:* Try using colored markers to put a mark or an asterisk on each stub—maybe red for medical expenses, yellow for charitable contributions, and so on—so that at the end of the year you can quickly go through your checkbook to pull together income tax information. Your personal computer can be a valuable tool for keeping track of all the checks you write and categorizing them automatically as well.

While you are thinking together about who is going to manage the money, you should at the same time start to put together your budget. The two considerations—who manages money and *how* you manage it—go hand in hand.

That machine in the wall

As a matter of fact, the ATM (Automatic Teller Machine) combined with EFT (Electronic Fund Transfer) and your PIN (Personal Identification Number) can take you right through the looking glass into the wonderland of the checkless society. You can, if you want, do all your banking without ever talking to or dealing with a teller. Make deposits, get cash, pay bills, transfer funds from one account to another—it's all possible with the ATM

Tips on using the ATM:

1. Enter every ATM transaction in your checkbook, the sooner the better. This is a *must*. If you find you are the type who just can't keep track of such things, do not use the ATM. Stick to plain old–fashioned check writing.
2. Take your receipt when the machine spits it out. Keep it in a safe place—a box or large envelope. It is your only record of the transaction.
3. If you are using EFT's, be sure to reconcile your bank statement. It is a) your proof of payment to the other party, b) your record for tax purposes, and c) your way of checking and reconciling those EFT transactions and your bank balance. If you find any discrepancy between your bank statement and your checkbook that results from an EFT, you must notify the bank within 60 days after your statement is mailed. If you fail to do so, and if the bank can show that it could have prevented the loss if you had contacted it, you may have to take the loss. In other words, the checkless society puts the burden of monitoring the system on you, the customer of the bank.
4. If you lose your ATM card or if you think it may have been stolen, you will be liable for no more than $50 of loss *if you contact the bank within two business days*. Otherwise you can be held responsible for losses up to $500.
5. Never lend anyone your ATM card. That's asking for trouble.

THE NICHOLSES USE A COMPUTER...

...to help manage their money. Before they were married, Eric and Jeanne Nichols spent a lot of time discussing their finances. "We did communicate and we still do so," says Eric. "We are paid weekly. We keep two checking accounts. I put all my paychecks and one of Jeanne's into one account. We pay all the bills out of this account. And this checkbook doesn't go out of the house. Jeanne deposits her other paychecks into a savings account and transfers to the other checking account what is needed for cash disbursements—food, drug store, gas and other daily living expenses. We use a computer program for both accounts. Each check is automatically categorized when we enter it. Sometimes it's tough to enter the cash disbursements, especially if one of us doesn't remember exactly how much went for food, for gas or for a movie. But this system works for us."

KAREN BUCK HANDLES THE HOUSEHOLD ACCOUNTS

As she says, "Pat always did a lot of traveling and didn't have the time. We have a joint account and we each keep separate accounts. He handles his expense–account money and the bills associated with his travel in his account. Mine is for my personal care, clothes, food and all the children's expenses. All of my salary goes into my account. Pat puts most of his paychecks into the joint account. And we use that account to handle all other bills. Every few months we sit down and go over the accounting."

WHAT PRICE CHILDREN?

4

There is no question but that one of the greatest joys in life is to raise a family.

There is also no question but that you must face some financial realities connected with having children.

Figures on what it costs to raise a child vary widely. The experts say that the cost of bringing up a child from birth to age 18 may range anywhere from $150,000 to $250,000. Add to that the cost of four years in a private residential college and it will take another $150,000 for a child born in 1990 and graduating from college in 2011, at the age of 22.

You could spend more. You could spend less. It all depends on your family, lifestyle, taste and goals. One consolation: A second or third child does not mean you must double or triple the costs, as the expenses seem to slide upward. Two do not cost a great deal more than one, except for such basics as getting born.

A birth is expensive. It can currently run about $2,500. Presumably you will have medical insurance to cover it. But make good and sure, *before* pregnancy occurs, that your insurance covers pregnancy, because once it is under way there is no way in the world you can delay the course of nature or backdate your insurance policy. Blue Cross, for example, has an 11–month waiting period, from the start of your coverage, before you can claim maternity benefits.

One of the first things to think about is whether your medical insurance will cover the birth of your child. The arrival of a child is probably one of the largest medical bills a young couple faces. Yet—surprisingly enough—most couples never check out the maternity benefits on their medical policies. The average cost, based on a three-day stay in the hospital for a routine birth, is $2,500—but the tab can run as high as $4,500 in some parts of the country. If the birth is by Caesarean section, the costs will be even higher. Generally speaking, the cost of having a baby is increasing faster than inflation.

There are some ways to save. Some hospitals offer to reduce costs if your pregnancy is low–risk by reducing your stay or by providing a birthing room, where you go through labor, delivery and recovery in the same bed. Then there are birth centers that stand apart from any hospital—but a birthing center has ties to a hospital in case of emergency. Still another way to save is to use a certified nurse–midwife for the delivery.

Before you start a pregnancy, check your maternity benefits. Too many couples have faced hospital bills that are not covered by their insurance. Find out:

1. What specific benefits are covered? Prenatal care, genetic testing, circumcision? Does your policy cover delivery at a birthing center?
2. What deductibles and what amount of co–payment are you responsible for? In other words, what are your out–of–pocket costs?
3. What if there are complications? Are you covered for a Caesarean birth, for example?
4. Under your policy, exactly when does coverage of the baby begin? What if the baby has to be in the intensive–care nursery?

KAREN'S PREGNANCIES WERE COVERED UNDER PAT'S MEDICAL PLAN AT WORK...

...through a comprehensive plan provided by a commercial insurance company. They had a choice of three basic comprehensive plans—the 100 Medical Plan, the 300 Medical Plan and the 500 Medical Plan. The only difference is the amount of the deductible ($100, $300 or $500) and maximum out–of–pocket expenses ($500, $1,500 or $2,500 per person). There is a maximum of three deductibles per family, and the maximum out–of–pocket is three times the individual. Thus, under the 100 Medical Plan, Karen and Pat have a maximum deductible of $300 with an out–of–pocket limit of $1,500. The deductible and their 20 percent co–payment are included in the maximum out–of–pocket. "We had checked this all out and knew we would have to come up with $1,500," says Pat. "Karen was working, so we made sure we had a separate account for the medical expenses. We started 'baby' accounts as soon as each pregnancy was confirmed."

But there are many people who do not have the benefits of a group plan. If you are buying an individual policy, there is usually a price for including maternity coverage—and a waiting period before the coverage starts.

VALERIE AND JAMES ARE SELF-EMPLOYED...

They had to find an individual medical policy. Their $1,000,000 Major Medical policy offers an optional deductible of $250, $500 or $1,000. The premium depends on the age of each spouse and the amount of the deductible. They chose the $500 deductible and currently pay about $60 per month. While they must pay the deductible—the first $500 of claims each year—the policy pays 80 percent of the next $5,000 of covered expenses for each calendar year—then 100 percent of the remaining covered expenses, up to a $1,000,000 maximum. Maternity, however, is an extra. The policy offers an optional pregnancy coverage with one of the following *maximum* benefit amounts: $500, $750 or $1,000. During the first benefit year, the plan will pay up to 50 percent of the maximum benefit amount, up to 75 percent of the maximum benefit amount during the second benefit year and 100 percent of the maximum benefit amount in all succeeding years. These pregnancy benefits must be in effect before the pregnancy begins. The $1,000 maximum benefit amount can cost nearly $30 more per month. With the average birth costing $2,500, this individual type of policy provides very little coverage. In the first year, the cost would be about $360 for the $1,000 maximum benefit. But remember—the policy pays only 50 percent of the maximum amount (or $500) if you give birth in the first year. If you have this type of coverage, you need to do some real saving for the birth of a child.

A BABY DOESN'T KNOW WHAT SCHEDULE YOU HAVE IN MIND

I know one couple who hadn't planned on the wife becoming pregnant. But when she did, the dates looked OK. Under their insurance, she would be covered after April 1, and the baby wasn't due until the middle of May. But Michael decided to arrive prematurely on March 28—four days before the insurance went into effect. Because he was premature, he was kept in the hospital for several weeks. In the four days before the insurance became effective, he cost his parents $4,000. After April 1 the insurance company picked up another $3,000 for his hospital costs.

You'll have other "first child" costs, too: nursery furniture, baby clothes, car seat, carriage, stroller, bottles and special dishes, toys and a million and one other things.

After the initial costs in the first few months, you can get lulled into a false sense of security. Costs don't generally rise much until your child starts school at the age of five. If Mom worked before the birth and is now staying home, however, your budget will be down by the amount of her former income. And when she goes back to work, you will have child-care costs to worry about.

Today it often takes two incomes to support a family. That means that paying for child care has become a way of life for a majority of young parents. For most of them, that way of life is also a major expense. And, for many, it is also an emotional issue—especially with the first child.

Child-care services range widely—from exchanging services with a friend to paying for a full-time nanny. The professional child-care services go by such charming names as Magic Kingdom, Sugar Plum Nursery, Tiny Tot Day Care, Happy Hour or Honey Bear—probably to endear themselves more to the parents than to the children.

Child care can be found in many different forms:

1. *In-home care.* Child care is provided in the home of the child by a babysitter who comes in by the day or by someone who lives in. The outside person may be a family member, a friend, a babysitter, a nanny or a young woman who works in exchange for room and board ("au pair").

2. *Family day-care homes.* Child care is provided in the home of the person who takes care of the children. If the home care is for more than a certain number of children, state or local laws or regulations may require that the home be licensed. Some states have strict requirements that involve on-site inspection and a minimum ratio of staff to children. Others require only that the home fill out an application and pay a fee. You'll find that many homes are licensed and that many are not.

3. *Child-care centers.* In these, child care is provided for a large number of children at a location within the community. The location may be a church, a converted school or a YWCA. Many day-care centers operate as independent businesses, while others are franchised centers. This type of center is usually staffed by teachers who have been trained in childhood education, with teachers aides as assistants.

4. *Worksite child care.* Child care is provided at or near the work place—often with the space provided by the employer, who may also pick up the expense of the maintenance and utilities. Worksite centers are usually run as non-profit organizations, with parents taking active roles in setting policy. Worksite child care is expanding as more and more companies are helping workers who have young dependents. Fees are usually on a sliding scale basis.

5. *Before- and after-school care.* Often operated by a child-care center, the local school district or a community or church-based organization, this provides supervision for children before and after school hours.

If you are going to place an infant in a day-care center, you should start looking before the child is born. Infant care that's just right for you can be hard to find, and the place you want may have a waiting list. When you find a place that seems right, ask for the names of three or four parents who have children in that program. Check them for their experience and opinion.

What to look for?

1. *Licensing.* Is the child-care facility licensed by the state? Find out about licensing and registration requirements.

2. *Eligibility.* At what age are the children accepted?

Infants (birth to two years old)
Toddlers (two to four years old)
Pre–school (four to five years old)
School age (for before and after care)

3. *Location.* Where is the child–care facility? How near to work, home, school?

4. *Time of operation.* What are the days and hours of operation? Can you get from work to pick up your child before the facility closes? Is it open evenings, on weekends, holidays and during the summer? Are there extra charges if you're late picking up your child?

5. *Fees.* Flat fee, sliding scale, special discount for more than one child, additional fees? What happens if you need care only on a part–time basis? Is financial aid available?

6. *Staff.* Are they certified by the state? What's their educational level and training? Employment history? That's just the beginning. What are the quality and interests of the teachers and aides? How do they interact with the children? Are they warm, loving, responsive—and patient? Do they guide and play with the children or do you sense that your child may get only custodial care? Notice how they communicate with the children. Are they good listeners? Do they take time to talk with each child? Can you sense that they show respect for the child's feelings, fostering a sense of self–esteem? Don't forget to check the staff–to–child ratio by age groups and ask about the turnover rates for the teachers and aides. If you find frequent turnover of staff, find out why. And finally, does the day–care facility have adequate liability insurance coverage?

7. *Health and safety.* Check with the local agency responsible for health and safety to find out whether the facility has been inspected for safe equipment, lead–free paint, safety of electrical system, fire exits and fire preparedness. Do the electrical outlets have safety plugs? Are there bars or gates on all windows above the first floor? Are there exposed nails? Are there gates to prevent toddlers from falling down stairs? Is the outside play area fenced in? If there is a kitchen, is it child–proof? And clean? Are the bathrooms accessible to children? Are there child–size toilets or potty chairs? How clean is the bathroom?

8. *Equipment.* Are there cribs for infants? Enough toys, cots, pillows, child–size desk and tables? Is the playground well equipped with swings, sand box, slides and running space? How well supervised is it?

9. *Decorations.* Are the decorations designed for children? Is the children's artwork hung at a child's eye level? Is it recent or current artwork?

10. *Meals and snacks.* Are they provided as part of the fee, or is there an extra charge? Check the menus. Are the meals and snacks nutritious? What if your child is on a special diet? Are the children allowed to help prepare the food? How are the meals served?

Many things to think of. Visit several programs. Get the feel of each place. Go see the same facility several times—but at different times of the day. Learn to follow your instincts in asking questions and looking searchingly at the place where your child may be spending the majority of his or her waking hours.

VALERIE AND JAMES'S LITTLE BOY, TAYLOR...

...is a "drop in" baby. Since his parents are musicians, their schedule can vary quite a bit. Usually, they need child care in the evening. They are fortunate to have a neighbor who watches their Taylor some evenings, and James's niece is also available on weekends when they are at work. During the day, Valerie has a part–time job, and when James isn't available she takes Taylor to a day–care facility. "But it can be difficult at the last minute because the place may be full on the particular afternoon when I need it. I've found that many facilities don't take children on a part–time or drop–in basis. But after some checking around, I did find a couple of places that take drop–ins. They charge by the hour. One of them didn't appeal to me. It always smells like a movie theater, with that buttery popcorn smell. But I have to say this—when I listen to other mothers, I realize how fortunate I am to have James around so much and to have family and friends who'll help while we're performing."

KAREN WENT BACK TO WORK...

...when Landon was one year old. She was lucky; she was working only part time, and she was able to leave Landon with a mother of five who took in a few other children. The expense was minimal, because the woman charged her only an hourly fee for the time that Landon was there.

When Landon was three, Megan was born and the Bucks moved near a large metropolitan area. Karen had to return to a full–time job just to make ends meet. At Town Hall she obtained a list of all licensed day–care centers in the town. The big shocker was the cost. Karen found that full–time care in a metropolitan area would cost about three times what it had cost in Des Moines. She began making calls, and networking finally put her in touch with a day–care facility called Magic Kingdom. The same woman has run this program for many years. She hires professional teachers for the preschool and kindergarten children, and her kindergarten curriculum is recognized by the state. There are only 15 children in Landon's class, and the children are taken to the local Y on Monday, Wednesday and Friday for gymnastics. Megan is in a small group of two–year–olds.

Next year, when Landon is in first grade, Karen will drop him off at his public school in the morning, and the school bus will take him from there to Magic Kingdom in the afternoon. He'll be able to do this through third grade. The flat fee will be less than the amount she has been paying for the preschool and kindergarten years. The biggest problem is that the children must be picked up from Magic Kingdom by 6:00 p.m. each afternoon and this can really cause some rushing. "I pray that I don't hit a traffic jam on my way home," says Karen, as Magic Kingdom imposes a hefty charge if a parent is late. Then comes summer: The facility is closed for one month, so she must arrange back–up care. "We take our vacation for two weeks and my mom flies in for the other two weeks. And in the middle of the winter, if school is closed because of snow but the Magic Kingdom is open, I have to pay."

Your vacation and the facility's vacation are probably not the same. But, in most instances, that space is reserved for you and you will be expected to pay the weekly fee.

What about day care right at the public school? Many children who are already in school need early morning and late afternoon day–care programs. "Latchkey" child–care services for them are growing faster than any other kind of day care. Many communities are setting up their own programs or contracting for them by setting them up in public schools. The idea is to expand the schools' hours and keep them open all year long in order to provide quality day care for older children. The advantage of this type of program is that the child stays right in the school building. The parent does not have to worry about the child being transported from school to somewhere else for an after–school program. Fees are either hourly, daily or weekly. Probably such programs will soon be expanded to include care of preschool children.

Many companies offer a Dependent Care Assistance Plan—a salary reduction program in which employees can use pre–tax dollars to pay for child–care expenses. The employer withholds up to $5,000 per year, the maximum allowed by the IRS, from the employee's salary. The employee pays for child care, and the company reimburses him or her from the money withheld. Karen is hoping that Pat's company will start such a program. She says, "It would save on taxes but it would really help with budgeting. The money would be deducted from the paycheck and set aside for child–care expenses. It couldn't be spent on other things."

And remember the tax credit for child care...

Paying for child care may qualify you for a tax credit that can reduce your tax liability. To qualify for the credit you must incur child-care expenses for children under 13 years old. For a married couple, both spouses must work full- or part- time.

The most you may figure the credit on is $2,400 a year in expenses for one qualifying dependent or $4,800 a year for two or more qualifying persons. The amount of the credit is a percentage of expenses you paid during the year and your employment income. For families with adjusted gross incomes of less than

$10,000, a 30 percent credit may be claimed for child–care expenses. With an adjusted gross income over $10,000 the 30 percent credit is reduced by 1 percent for each $2,000 of adjusted gross income, but not below 20 percent. The 20 percent limit is for those with an adjusted gross income over $28,000. The maximum credit for a couple with one child and an adjusted gross income of $28,000 is $480 (20 percent of $2,400).

To claim the child–care credit, you'll have to provide the name, address and Social Security number of the care provider to the IRS. You will not be able to take the credit if you do not pay Social Security tax on the wages you pay a child–care provider.

Rising expenses from age five

By the time your first child enters nursery school or kindergarten, you will be patching jeans and buying new shoes every few months. But after the first day of school, you will realize that old clothes are in. You may want your daughter to look neat and sparkling clean, but you are likely to find clay in pockets, sand in shoes, and a creative finger paint design all over an only–this–morning–all–white T–shirt.

With first grade come countless activities outside the house. Soon there are guitar lessons, Little League, special art classes, ballet, swimming at the Y, and—when there is a spare moment—just plain going to Jane's or Fred's house after school. All this may mean miles of very short local auto trips—and up goes the budget for gasoline. The lessons add to the budget, too, and entail buying equipment (ballet slippers, musical instruments, art supplies).

Tip: If music lessons are begun, always check the possibilities of renting the musical instrument, at least for the first few months, until you are sure there is really a strong interest in continuing to play it. But find a way to rent without throwing cold water on the idea of playing and without casting doubts on your child's ability, talent, or interest.

Through the elementary school years, appetites grow, and so do arms and legs and feet. Clothes are outgrown faster than you can wash them. Video games are a must. Day camp first, and then a regular summer camp that makes heavy demands ($3,000 per summer, on average). You can spend weeks sewing name tags on a thousand T–shirts, shorts, socks, towels, sheets, sweaters, and you–name–it, and lay out big bucks for books, sleeping bag, canteen, camera, tennis racket, baseball glove, or whatever—only to find, four to six weeks later, that half the wardrobe went home in someone else's trunk and the other half is so worn and dirty that the clothes must simply be junked. And where is the tennis racket? The camera? The baseball glove?

Now comes the orthodontist. With more and more companies providing some insurance that covers costs of braces for employees' youngsters, you may luck out on this one. For many families, it has always been a big expense in the subteen and early teenage years. Since you have 10 or 12 years before this cost can hit you, you have time to (1) check insurance plans and maybe even lobby for this kind of coverage where you work if you are not getting it, (2) include it in your savings goals, and (3) hope the two of you have brought together the right genes so there will be no overbite or other such problem.

Even without big dental bills, the teenage years can be a financial disaster area. Clothes? They are expensive. And for some reason or other, the teenager is convinced that a lot of them are needed. If a spot doesn't *come* out, the shirt *goes* out. Hair is washed at least once a day and blow–dried, so electric bills soar (if your child isn't using the hair drier, a friend is). Suddenly there are no *off* switches on the TV or stereo or lights. I can remember coming home to see the entire house ablaze with lights and shaking with sound, and, on entering, screaming, "Turn off the damn stereo and TV," only to find there was no one at home.

Your food budget is likely to zoom, too. There is no such thing as a leftover after hordes of teenagers descend on your refrigerator. The bag of Oreos, the pound of cold cuts, the six–pack of Coke that were meant to last a week—all are gone in an afternoon.

Out of sheer desperation, you may decide to install a "children's phone," with its own number and listing in the phone book. This can help relieve you of having to listen to giggling on the phone for hours on end, not to mention the fact that no one is able to get through to you.

Who is paying for all this? Probably you are. But you can get some help from—of all people—your kids. Many a teenager pays or helps pay for the children's phone with income from baby–sitting, and many help out with their clothes budgets. It's a good chance, too, for you to lay the groundwork for their own thinking about financial planning, and handling money. In fact, you should be sure to start such thinking the first time you reach into your pocket to hand out allowance money—probably late in kindergarten year, when the values of coins will have become established, and certainly some time in the first grade. (The value of money is pretty vague to children five years old or less. Kindergartners often think a dollar is good pay for a day's work, or that $100 is a fair price for a sack of potatoes. When they play store, they *always* insist on giving you change—because their concept of money is manipulative rather than numerical. Over the kindergarten year, their concept changes.)

The biggie of the teenage years is the driver's license. If your child happens to be male, along with the license comes an auto insurance bill that is probably double what it was before. And the teenager no longer has legs—he or she has wheels. You decide to go out one evening, only to run out of gas. But you know you filled the tank last night and you haven't driven the car since then.

"But Mom, I put in gas."

"How much?"

"A dollar's worth."

And your kid may be ready to raise the hood and apply what's been learned from an article in *Popular Mechanics* to servicing your car. Then there are the minor dents that the insurance doesn't cover. And the possibility of a major accident that the insurance *will* pay for. (Billy, my neighbor's son, totaled his mother's car the day he got his license. Luckily, he knew what seat belts were for.)

New technology and changes in our culture will introduce new wants and needs that neither I nor anyone else can predict. My own children got through the teenage years before the computer and the video game arrived in the family room. While you can remember when such hardware came in and how you made it commonplace, your children will think the world always had computers for everybody—and their teenage demands for the latest thing will reach even further. It is really very difficult to give you any specific figures on the cost of having children. There are just too many ifs, ands, and buts. If one parent stays home to raise the children…if you both work through their childhoods but have the costs of child care, more taxes, commuting, two business wardrobes rather than one, and laundry service or a cleaning person…if you have two kids…if you have three…

The important thing is not to let dollar signs get in the way. True, raising a family will cost a small fortune. But how often did that ever stop anybody from raising a family? Children are priceless. Their cost is meaningless. You will know that—and you'll remember it—the first time your child gives you a hug and says, "Thank you." And that can happen many, many times over.

The child-rearing years pass like a summer storm. I know. Let me be blunt about it by sharing with you a letter I wrote to my daughter soon after she was married. I said:

You children have been the biggest pain in the ass—yet you've been the greatest source of satisfaction—in my life. My greatest accomplishment has been being a mother. Everything else has been secondary.

COST OF EDUCATION

5

One of the most common financial errors that young parents make is their failure to plan ahead for their children's education. You need to calculate future college expenses. The future costs will depend on the annual cost in today's dollars, inflation and the ages of your children.

Tuition at a private college will probably cost you more than anything you will ever purchase, except a home. College costs have skyrocketed since 1980. Tuition has been increasing by a minimum of at least 6 percent a year, almost doubling college costs every 10 years.

So if you wait until your child is in high school to start a fund for education, it is bound to be too little and too late. Just take a look at what it can cost.

To find the factor by which inflation will increase college costs over the years, see Exhibit 3. Find the number of years until your child starts college and then find the inflation factor.

Scary, isn't it? It would be so easy to bury your head in the sand and hope the money for college will come out of thin air. Well, that's not going to happen. "But we'll get financial aid," say some people. You

will find it hard to get enough. Federal student grants cannot keep up with the increasing costs of higher education. In addition, government funds for college grants and loans have been cut. The elimination of tax advantages for minor children has also made it harder and more expensive to save for education.

The Tax Reform Act of 1986 eliminated certain tax advantages for minor children, creating what has become known as the "kiddie tax." Before tax reform, a child could earn $1,080 from interest or dividends tax–free. Any investment income over that amount was taxed at the child's rate. Now, for children under 14, the first $500 is tax–free and the second $500 is taxed at the child's rate. If the unearned income (interest and dividend income) is more than $1,000, it is taxed at the parent's rate, regardless of the source of income. At a 9 percent return, more than $5,000 can be held in an account before any of the unearned income will be taxed. Unearned income for children over 14 is still taxed at the child's rate.

If you have children under 14, you should think in terms of tax–deferred investments or fast–growing stocks. If taxation on investment returns can be

Exhibit 3
INFLATION FACTOR

The current yearly rate of college inflation is 6% according to the College Board. To find the factor by which inflation will increase college costs over the years, select the appropriate figure in the left column and find the inflation factor to the right.

Years to Start of College	Factor: Rate of Inflation (6%)	Years to Start of College	Factor: Rate of Inflation (6%)
1	1.06	10	1.80
2	1.12	11	1.91
3	1.19	12	2.02
4	1.26	13	2.14
5	1.34	14	2.27
6	1.42	15	2.41
7	1.51	16	2.55
8	1.60	17	2.70
9	1.70	18	2.87

Source: Fidelity Investments

deferred, it is likely that the funds will grow at higher after–tax rates. U.S. Government Series EE Bonds are an example of a tax–deferred savings vehicle. If you hold the bonds for more than five years, the interest is tax deferred until you redeem them. The trick here is to make sure that the bonds you purchase will mature after your child reaches age 14.

Another tax–deferred investment is zero coupon bonds. These are bonds that have been stripped of their interest coupons. The bonds can be corporate bonds, treasury bonds or municipal bonds. Interest is paid when the bond matures or is "called." The problem is that you must pay taxes yearly on the income earned, even though you don't receive the income directly. So invest in municipal zero coupon bonds because municipal bond interest is not taxable. But, remember to work it out so the bonds will mature when the first tuition bill is due.

Fast–growing stocks or mutual funds are another investment for the child under age 14. Here, you are buying into investments that have great growth

potential over the years but currently do not pay much in dividends. (More on these in Chapter 12 on investments.) When your child reaches 14, these investments can be sold and the proceeds put in safe high–yielding investments. Another tax–deferred investment to consider: a whole or universal life insurance policy. In these, you invest in a life insurance policy, letting the earnings accumulate. While they are accumulating, you pay no federal or state tax on the earnings. When your child turns 14, you can withdraw the accumulated earnings and invest the money in your child's name. Or if you would rather not turn the funds over to your child, pay the tuition bills from the policy's tax–free earnings.

Besides the type of saving or investment, you must think about how you want the accounts set up. Parents or grandparents can set up custodial accounts under the Uniform Gifts to Minors Act (UGMA). The custodian is responsible for managing the funds until the child reaches maturity—usually at age 18. Remember that if the child is under 14, the account can earn up to $1,000 in interest tax–free. This type of account has one major drawback: Once the child reaches age 18, the child can do whatever she or he wants with the money—be it go to college, buy a flashy sports car or take a trip around the world.

But you can consider setting up a trust under Section 2503(c) of the 1986 Tax Code. The trustee, usually a parent, has complete control over the income and principal until the child reaches age 21. The trust pays income taxes at its own rate, thereby avoiding the age 14 "kiddie tax" rule. This means that the first $5,000 of income in the trust is taxed at the 15 percent rate. Amounts over $5,000 are taxed at the 28 percent rate.

Some universities are coming up with their own ideas for helping parents foot the education bills. Some arrange for a parent to buy future tuitions in one lump sum at a discounted cost—"pay now, attend later" or "tuition future" plans. The discounted cost is based on when the student will enter and what the college believes it can earn between now and then. The interest is supposed to make up the difference between the current tuition and what will be charged in the future. One problem is that if your child decides not to go to that college, you might be refunded only your original investment, with the college keeping all the earnings. If the school cannot earn sufficient return on the investment to meet future costs, it will have to come up with the shortfall. Because of spiraling education costs and the changes in interest rates, uncertainty about these plans is growing. And to allow for a quicker response to changes in the financial markets, many contracts are set quarterly rather than annually.

Many banks have savings plans designed for college savings. Here's a type of prepayment plan that can be used at any school: The bank sells certificates of deposit based on the average tuition rates at various groups of schools, and guarantees that investment income will keep up with rising college costs. Because college costs have been rising faster than inflation, an up-front premium of several thousand dollars is required.

There will probably be several changes in the tax laws between now and the time when your children attend college. And new ways to invest are sure to come along for parents who are wise enough to be saving for college costs. Keep an eye on what is happening in the world of saving for education. And when your child reaches high–school age, learn all there is to know about financial aid.

The lowest cost of funding is an immediate lump–sum transfer of money to your children. The younger they are, the less you have to put away, as the funds will have a longer period in which to grow. But most young couples do not have money to set aside in one lump sum.

Now that you have an idea of what it is going to cost to send your child to college, you'll need to figure out how much you will need to invest each year and the yield you will need to earn to meet that goal. To determine the factor by which a 10 percent rate of return, compounded annually, increases your investment, find the number of years until your child starts and find the return rate factor.

LANDON BUCK HAS 13 YEARS BETWEEN NOW AND THE TIME HE ENTERS COLLEGE...

Karen and Pat filled out the college worksheet on page 31 and discovered to their amazement that the future cost of educating Landon would be about

Exhibit 4
RETURN RATE FACTOR

While no one can predict the future value of an investment, you must assume some rate of return to estimate your investment target. To determine the factor by which a 10% rate of return, compounded annually, increases your investment, select the appropriate figure from the left column and find the return rate factor to the right.

Years to Start of College	Factor: Rate of Return (10%)	Years to Start of College	Factor: Rate of Return (10%)
1	1.00	10	15.94
2	2.10	11	18.53
3	3.31	12	21.38
4	4.64	13	24.52
5	6.10	14	27.98
6	7.71	15	31.77
7	9.49	16	35.95
8	11.43	17	40.55
9	13.58	18	45.60

Source: Fidelity Investments

$85,600 in today's dollars, assuming an annual cost today of $10,000.

They also figured out the lump sums they would have to put away today, using a present–value factor (see Exhibit 5, page 30). In 13 years, the present–value factor is 0.368, figuring an 8 percent return. A lump–sum transfer would require about $31,500 (0.368 × $85,600 with an 8 percent annual return) or $24,824 (0.290 × $85,600 with a 10 percent annual return). A lump–sum transfer for Megan would require about $22,236 (0.218 × $102,000 with a 10 percent annual return).

Since Karen and Pat do not have the funds to make a lump–sum investment for education, they then used the worksheet to help them figure out the amount they would have to save on a monthly basis. The monthly amount needed is $290 for Landon and $236 for Megan. They decided to use a growth mutual fund and have the fund withdraw $300 each month from

Exhibit 5
PRESENT VALUE FACTOR OF $1 BY % RETURN

Year	1%	2%	3%	4%	5%	6%	7%	8%	9%	10%
1	0.990	0.980	0.971	0.962	0.952	0.943	0.935	0.926	0.917	0.909
2	0.980	0.961	0.943	0.925	0.907	0.890	0.873	0.857	0.842	0.826
3	0.971	0.942	0.915	0.889	0.864	0.840	0.816	0.794	0.772	0.751
4	0.961	0.924	0.888	0.855	0.823	0.792	0.763	0.735	0.708	0.683
5	0.951	0.906	0.863	0.822	0.784	0.747	0.713	0.681	0.650	0.621
6	0.942	0.888	0.837	0.790	0.746	0.705	0.666	0.630	0.596	0.564
7	0.933	0.871	0.813	0.760	0.711	0.665	0.623	0.583	0.547	0.513
8	0.923	0.853	0.789	0.731	0.677	0.627	0.582	0.540	0.502	0.467
9	0.914	0.837	0.766	0.703	0.645	0.592	0.544	0.500	0.460	0.424
10	0.905	0.820	0.744	0.676	0.614	0.558	0.508	0.463	0.422	0.386
11	0.896	0.804	0.722	0.650	0.585	0.527	0.475	0.429	0.388	0.350
12	0.887	0.788	0.701	0.625	0.557	0.497	0.444	0.397	0.356	0.319
13	0.879	0.773	0.681	0.601	0.530	0.469	0.415	0.368	0.326	0.290
14	0.870	0.758	0.661	0.577	0.505	0.442	0.388	0.340	0.299	0.263
15	0.861	0.743	0.642	0.555	0.481	0.417	0.362	0.315	0.275	0.239
16	0.853	0.728	0.623	0.534	0.458	0.394	0.339	0.292	0.252	0.218
17	0.844	0.714	0.605	0.513	0.436	0.371	0.317	0.270	0.231	0.198
18	0.836	0.700	0.587	0.494	0.416	0.350	0.296	0.250	0.212	0.180
19	0.828	0.686	0.570	0.475	0.396	0.331	0.277	0.232	0.194	0.164
20	0.820	0.673	0.554	0.456	0.377	0.312	0.258	0.215	0.178	0.149

their checking account. "What we don't see, we won't spend on something else," says Pat. "This is a painless way of saving and making sure that the money will be there for Landon's education." To cover the educational expenses for Megan, they plan to increase the amount they are saving when they get salary increases. "We also feel by the time we need to pay for education, we will have built up substantial equity in our home, whether we are living here or some place else. If we haven't saved enough we can borrow on the house."

Worksheet II: The Bucks
COST OF COLLEGE EDUCATION

What will college cost? To estimate how much college will cost, and how much is needed to invest to meet the target, complete the following worksheet.

	Child's Name Landon	Child's Name Megan
1. Enter your child's age	5	2
2. Years to college; time to invest (18 minus child's age)	13	16
3. Annual college costs* a. Enter your own estimate or b. $6,000, public school c. $10,000, private school	$10,000	$10,000
4. College Inflation Factors: According to the College Board, college costs are increasing 6% per year. Refer to Exhibit 3 for the inflation factor based on your time horizon.	2.14	2.55
5. Future annual cost of college Step 3 × Step 4	$21,400	$25,500
6. Future total cost of college Step 5 × number of years of college	$85,600	$102,000

*According to the College Board, these are approximate annual costs of public and private colleges for the 1986–1987 school year.

How much should I invest?

7. Assumed rate of return (10%)** Take the number of years your child has until college, refer to Exhibit 4, and enter applicable return rate factor	24.52	35.95
8. Annual target amount to invest Divide Step 6 by Step 7	$3,490	$2,837
9. Monthly amount to invest Divide Step 8 by 12	$291	$236

**Assumed 10% rate of return. This is the average rate of return of the S & P 500 for the 20 years ended 6/30/87. Source: Fidelity Investments.

Worksheet II: Yours
COST OF COLLEGE EDUCATION

What will college cost? To estimate how much college will cost, and how much is needed to invest to meet the target, complete the following worksheet.

	Child's Name	Child's Name
1. Enter your child's age		
2. Years to college; time to invest (18 minus child's age)		
3. Annual college costs* a. Enter your own estimate or b. $6,000, public school c. $10,000, private school		
4. College Inflation Factors: According to the College Board, college costs are increasing 6% per year. Refer to Exhibit 3 for the inflation factor based on your time horizon.		
5. Future annual cost of college Step 3 × Step 4		
6. Future total cost of college Step 5 × number of years of college		

*According to the College Board, these are approximate annual costs of public and private colleges for the 1986–1987 school year.

How much should I invest?

7. Assumed rate of return (10%)** Take the number of years your child has until college, refer to Exhibit 4, and enter applicable return rate factor		
8. Annual target amount to invest Divide Step 6 by Step 7		
9. Monthly amount to invest Divide Step 8 by 12		

**Assumed 10% rate of return. This is the average rate of return of the S & P 500 for the 20 years ended 6/30/87. Source: Fidelity Investments.

HOW TO MANAGE THE MONEY: YOUR BUDGET

6

Nobody likes the terms *cash flow* or *budget*. They mean discipline. They mean harsh reality. They mean a very firm "yes" or "no" when you are considering an expenditure. Cash–flow analysis is not as harsh a term. What you are really doing is analyzing what is coming in and what is going out. The reason is to get a handle on how you are spending and allocating your resources.

Whether you use the term budget or cash flow, nothing is more important in a family. If one of the two paychecks is temporary, start right now and try to live on just one income. Salt away the other. If you have recently had a child and have left the work–force, did you save enough to allow you to do this? Or, by living on one income, are things tighter than you expected? If you returned to work after the birth of a child, did you "budget in" the cost of child care and all those other expenses.

In fact, even if you think both incomes are "permanent," don't spend them both up to the limit. There are too many unpredictables out there: a temporary layoff, a disability, any number of unforeseen expenses.

What is a budget?

A budget is a worksheet. A road map. A resume. It depicts your lifestyle and shows what you need to do to manage it. It shows you how to get to where you want to be.

The fun of it is that you make your own rules. Want a vacation next year without the baby? Budget for it. Want a VCR so you can watch those movies that you are now missing? Budget for it. Want a cam-recorder to make videos of the baby? Budget for it. Want to step out more often to the movies or theater without the children? Budget for additional babysitting.

The point is that the money is yours. No one can tell anyone else how to spend their money. *You* decide on the priorities that will make *your* lifestyle.

Your budget—a road map

Think of your budget as just that: a road map. Its purpose is to show you where you are going and how to get there. But it can be used, like any good road map, to show you where you can *sensibly* and safely get off the road when you must, then get back on again without losing direction or missing your destination. It is important for you both to realize that you can do that. You can change your route to cope with an emergency or a change in plans that may delay reaching your planned destination. There's nothing wrong with that if you do have your map to guide you and remind you of your goal and the route you structured for reaching it.

Your budget is valuable not only as a road map. It is the key to knowing how much credit you can safely afford to carry. Millions of Americans constantly face the problem of paying for what they bought yesterday while feeling the urge to buy something more today. Only a well–tended budget can answer the nagging question, can we afford the payments?

Every budget has two sides

Getting and spending. Income and outgo. Revenue and expenses. Every budget has two sides, one for money arriving, the other for money departing. The two sides are basic to every budget in creation—a household budget for two of you, or the budget of a giant transnational corporation with worldwide production, employees and sales.

Start with your revenue budget. (See Worksheet III on page 50, headed **Sources of Income**.)

On this sheet, for each of you, write down *all* your income, by category: what you earn as wages or salary; extra money you take in from part–time work, moonlighting, hobbies, whatever, interest you get from savings accounts; dividends from investments; regular gifts from parents; rent from any property you own or from roomers or boarders; payments from unemployment insurance or disability insurance. Look at your paycheck stub and note deductions for Social Security, taxes, and any fringe benefits.

Tip: Be brutally honest. Do not count un-hatched chickens. A pay raise is not a pay raise until it comes home in your paycheck. Your budget is always *now*. It is never what might be: what you hope it will be next month, or even what promises lead you to think it is going to be.

Now look at the expense side of your budget.

TIPS ON SOUND SPENDING HABITS

You can learn to spend your money efficiently and, as a result, save money. One of the key clues is knowing how to recognize the difference between your *needs* and your *wants*.

1. Watch the non–essentials. How much are you spending for a magazine you don't read, a milk shake, a taxi ride when the bus would get you there, seeing a movie you didn't want to see just because another couple was going?

2. Guard against sales. If you really need the item, buy it. If a blouse "was such a bargain, I couldn't resist," you may be in for adding a skirt or shoes to match. Note when certain items go on sale every year—January white sales, Christmas cards at half price right after the holidays (but don't buy them in January unless you really will use them the following December).

3. Never charge a sale item on a credit card on which you are making time payments. The finance charges will cost you what you saved on the sale.

4. Speaking of credit cards, you can save one or two annual credit card fees by simply eliminating one or two credit cards, if you already have more than a couple.

5. And speaking of fees—check out checking accounts. Find one that charges you *no* fees if you maintain a minimum balance, and then stay above that minimum.

6. Make shopping lists—and stick to them. The supermarkets thrive on impulse buying by people who don't have firm lists. Probably you seldom go to the grocery store without a list. But make lists for all other shopping, too. And be especially cautious about impulse buying when Junior is riding in the shopping cart.

7. Why buy tools that you don't often use? You can rent them more cheaply than owning them. Need a leaf blower once or twice a fall? Rent it. Ski once or twice a year? Rent the skis. You can find furniture, stereos, TV sets, plants, clothing, dishes, tableware—just about anything—for rent. Look in the telephone book yellow pages.

8. If you're in a neighborhood where a number of people could use a leaf blower or snow blower or a special lawn mower, buy it together. But be sure someone takes responsibility for maintenance.

9. Barter. Or swap services. You could babysit for a neighbor in exchange for a ride to work every day. You might change the oil in a neighbor's car as a trade for use of a lawn mower. You can think of a zillion ways to gain services by trading your own.

10. Speaking of barter—there's nothing wrong with trading your children's outgrown clothing for something that fits, as long as the clothing in both cases is clean and only outgrown, not outworn.

11. Avoid shopping with a friend. Especially with someone who makes more than you do or has different spending habits. A fancy shop where you would never go alone? And now you're in there buying something because your friend shops there? No way! Don't ever feel ashamed to say, "No, thanks."

12. Buy at discount stores. Look over ones near you. Some are better than others, in terms of the quality of the merchandise. All give you good price breaks.

13. Save your small change. Empty pockets or purse of all coins every night. You will fill a coffee can before you know it. Keep hands out of this pot and lug it to the savings bank. (Most savings banks have machines that will count up your coins in just a few minutes.)

14. Think energy when you think budget. Can you ride a bike or walk to work, and save on gasoline? Do you turn off the lights when you leave a room? Should you have a day–night thermostat installed?

15. Speaking of energy, do you really need to keep buying videotapes and recording all those ball games and old (or not–so–old) movies on your VCR? Come on, you couch potato!

16. Save on long–distance phone calls. Check your phone book for the difference in rates during various time periods. If you make a lot of long–distance calls, consider signing up with one of the budget long–distance companies.

17. Watch lunches out. If you are both working, keep a close eye on spending for pickup meals, whether fast–food or gourmet.

18. Think long–range savings. A microwave oven may or may not be a luxury. If you use it regularly to reheat leftovers that you would otherwise throw out, it could be worth the initial expense.

Two kinds of expenses: fixed and flexible

Fixed expenses are those you must pay regularly—every month or every quarter or once a year. They are expenses you cannot escape or change to any great degree; the rent or mortgage payment, insurance premiums, taxes, monthly payments on credit obligations, utilities. (Of course, you can reduce utility bills by disciplining telephone use, turning off lights, lowering the thermostat.)

To be sure you always have the money to pay these, make a payment every month to a *fixed–expenses account*. To determine how much you need for this account every month, line up all your fixed expenses for the year, writing them in on Worksheet IV (pages 51-53) for each month. Some you have to pay every month (rent or mortgage, for example), some quarterly (insurance premiums, probably), some semi–annually (real estate taxes), some annually (example: personal property taxes). Total each category, then figure out its monthly average. Now total the monthly averages to see how much must go into your fixed–expenses account each month. Hard as it will be—*at first*—you must start immediately to put in that amount every month. No matter how enticing the sale or how tight the money seems, you must fight off the urge to dip into your reserves for fixed expenses. (More in a moment on practical ways to handle the money—literally.) Be sure the checkbook for this account does not go to the market but stays home in the desk drawer. If you have direct deposit of your check, ask the bank to split your total take–home, putting that monthly average into your fixed–expense account. The balance goes to your flexible–expense account.

Once you have established the habit of putting that monthly average into the fixed–expenses account, you will find it is painless to maintain. With the system functioning well, you will always be able to pay a tax bill or the insurance premium when it comes due.

Think of *savings* as a fixed expense. The first kind of savings you need is a payment to yourselves for an *emergency fund.*

How much goes into it? At any one time, your emergency fund should contain the equivalent of three to six months' net income. If you are both working, if car and appliances and houses are new and not likely to cry for major repairs soon, it is safe to have a minimum of three months' income stashed away. Later on, especially as your family grows, you will feel a lot more comfortable when you maintain a six–month cushion for emergencies.

So figure how much your emergency fund should be, and start now to put it away.

After your emergency fund has built up to a safe level, be sure to keep replenishing it regularly.

Use this cash reserve for just that: emergencies. A major medical expense not covered by insurance, a major car or household repair, a stretch of unemployment—such emergencies, without the reserves on hand to pay for them, could send you to a bank or some other lender to sign for a loan. That, in turn, would add to your fixed obligations each month, giving you more to pay out, more to worry about, and less to have for flexible expenses and discretionary spending. Your savings each month should also include the amount you have determined is necessary to reach specific goals.

"Do we really need this?"

When you want to buy something, ask yourselves, "Do we really need this?" The question can help you control impulse buying. Having taken a good hard look at your priorities as you analyze your cash flow, you will find yourselves distinguishing between buying for pleasure and buying for need. By making this distinction every time you make a significant expenditure—and only you two know what's significant for you—you will stay financially fit.

> *Tip:* To test your real need to buy something, write out a check for its purchase. Look at the check. Do you need that amount now, to buy groceries or pay a department store bill? If you do, you don't need the item you are considering. Can you make up the amount by skipping several trips to the movies, putting off a holiday trip, not dining out a

few times? Better to do so than to make the purchase and then find out you cannot pay for basic flexible expenses or discover yourselves dipping into money you need for fixed expenses.

Of course, you have to make trade–offs. That's inevitable. But you can establish limits for large expenses. You can agree in advance that you won't spend more than a certain amount for a car or to furnish a room.

Above all, remember that money is not an end in itself. It is a tool to help you enjoy life and reach your goals. So spend realistically and save carefully in ways you can be comfortable with.

And let your budget be your guide—your road map. Review it at least once a year. See where it needs adjusting, where goals have been met, where new goals should be set. When you have successfully cut costs or gained a short–term goal, you can even reward yourselves with a special dinner out or—if the numbers are right—a weekend away.

IMPORTANT BUDGETING DON'TS

- Don't dictate. You must work out the budget together, with full mutual agreement.
- Don't rush. You can't work out a budget in one evening. It takes time. Go back to it after you have both thought about it.
- Don't go by what others spend (don't keep up with the Joneses).
- Don't look for miracles. Your budget is a management tool. It will not, all by itself, give you more money or cut your spending.
- Don't nickel–and–dime it. Round figures up or down to the nearest dollar, and big figures to the nearest ten dollars.
- Don't overdo the paperwork. Report the essentials, that's all.
- Don't be inflexible. Remember that a budget must have room for give and take. Circumstances will change. Income will grow, but so will outgo. Children will arrive. Interests will shift. Be ready to review, evaluate, revise, and adjust as your lifestyle changes.

Handling flexible expenses

What are flexible expenses? They are those you spend for regularly but that may vary in amount depending on what you're doing, how you're feeling, what you need. Food, of course. Clothing. Medical care. Cars and travel. (The cost of regular commuting by train, subway, or bus, however, is a fixed expense; it should be calculated in your fixed–expense total.) Entertainment and recreation. Ordinary household maintenance (such non–emergencies as cleaning services). Laundry and dry cleaning. Magazine subscriptions.

Tip: How to "handle" your money so you are fair to each part of your budget? The best way is to set up three separate bank accounts:

1. A savings account for your emergency fund.
2. A checking account for your fixed expenses. (Some people who have immense self–discipline find that they can keep their emergency–fund money and their fixed–expenses in the same account. I admire such Spartans, but I am not one of them. My recommendation: Set up separate accounts.)
3. A checking account for your flexible expenses. There's another system. People used to use it all the time. Some still do. It's the *envelope system.* It gives you immediate feedback, so you know where you stand. You mark envelopes for each of your basic flexible–expense items—food, entertainment, clothing, etc. Into each envelope you put the amount you have budgeted for that expense. If by the 20th of the month the entertainment envelope is empty, you know you have spent your budget and you watch TV. If the food envelope is empty by the 20th, you'll find yourself doing some frantic borrowing from other categories and you'll be more cautious in the supermarket next month. The chief disadvantage of the envelope system: You're keeping more cash in the house than it's wise to.

How much to budget per category?

How do you know how much to budget for each category of flexible expenses—especially if the two of you have not lived together before or budgeted before?

Your best guide is what you spent last year, if you kept records. If you did not keep records, start today to keep some.

Record keeping is easy. There are only three ways you can pay for something: with cash, by check when you buy it or by charge account paid later. Always get a receipt, whether you are paying by cash, check or charge. If you cannot get a receipt (not even a cash register tape), make your own note of date, item, and amount.

Put all receipts on a spindle at home—or in a large envelope, filed chronologically. When you pay by check, be sure to note on your checkbook stub for what (and for whom) the purchase was made.

In tallying charge accounts against your budget, be sure to categorize what is actually charged, not what you are paying on your total charge bill, as you may be paying it off in installments.

Now, total all the columns on your expense sheets (Worksheet IV). Are your total expenditures higher than your income? If they are, don't be discouraged. Overspending gives you a good reason for doing an analysis, taking a good hard look at priorities, cutting down here or there.

A TIGHT BUDGET IS A MUST FOR THE McQUARTERS

Income is never the same two weeks in a row—let alone month after month—for Valerie and James. As musicians, they not only see it rise and fall constantly, but they also have no sure way to base their budget for the future. So they took what they earned together in the previous year and made that the base for their budget in the next year.

Since they are both self–employed, they get *all* their pay. No employer does any withholding. That means they have to include income taxes and Social Security payments in the amounts they budget, and pay them quarterly on an estimated basis.

Before arriving at net earnings on which to base the payments of estimated taxes, they deduct all expenses related to their profession: musical instruments, telephone, automobile, costumes.

"Our fixed and flexible expenses come to a little over $20,000 a year," says James. "That's about $1,700 a month. We put all our paychecks into a savings account. Then we transfer $1,500 into our checking account every month—more if we have a big bill, like an insurance bill. The balance sits right in that money market account so it can earn some extra, and we use it to pay the taxes, buy the musical equipment we need, cover emergencies, and best of all, pay for the materials we need to finish the house. We won't touch those savings for anything we don't really have to have."

RENT IS THE NICHOLSES' BIG EXPENSE

For that reason, Jeanne and Eric Nichols put saving for their house into their budget from day one of their marriage. "We do enjoy eating out at a fine restaurant once a month," says Jeanne. "When you're in the food business, it's nice to have someone else wait on you once in a while. And it's a good way to get new ideas. Of course, since we both eat breakfast and lunch on the job, our food bill is minimal." Eric adds that they both wear uniforms at work, so there is no need for a closet full of clothes.

THE BUCKS FEEL A STRAIN...

...even with so much money coming in. Pat Buck is earning $61,000 a year. He puts 10 percent of his salary into a pre–tax—401(k)—plan. Karen Buck is earning $28,000.

The interest on their $200,000 mortgage, the property taxes, and four personal exemptions reduce the amount of income that is subject to Federal income taxes.

"We're just making it," says Karen. "Over 40 percent of our gross income goes to pay the mortgage, car loans and child care. We now go to discount stores for our clothes and we've cut our entertainment expenses down to about half of what they were before we moved here. We used to go to dinner and the theater quite often—but ticket prices now? Out of sight! We've cut down on dinners out. We rent movies—we're regular couch potatoes! Of course, I know a lot of money goes to picking up prepared dinners, but I just can't seem to cook every night. What I'd really love is household help—but that's impossible. But I do have a cleaning service come in twice or three times a year. It seems like we have so much money coming in but we live from paycheck to paycheck. If Pat stays here in corporate headquarters, he should get good promotions, with hefty raises. But then, one never knows."

Worksheet III: The McQuarters
SOURCES OF INCOME

	JAN	FEB	MARCH	APRIL	MAY	JUNE	JULY	AUG	SEPT	OCT	NOV	DEC	TOTAL
Valerie	75	50	85	125	125	130	95	100	120	115	100	400	1,520
James	200	150	150	400	250	800	250	500	400	700	400		4,200
Joint	1,200	2,000	1,700	2,000	3,500	2,500	1,800	1,750	1,200	900	2,500	3,000	24,050
Interest	40	40	40	40	40	40	40	40	40	40	40	40	480
Total	1,515	2,240	1,975	2,565	3,915	3,470	2,185	2,390	1,760	1,755	3,040	3,440	30,250

Worksheet III: The Nicholses
SOURCES OF INCOME

EARNED INCOME	Husband	Wife	Joint	Total	Monthly
Wages/Salary	29,000	30,000		59,000	4,917
Self-Employment Income					
Bonus					
INVESTMENT INCOME					
Interest/Savings			500	500	42
Interest/Bonds					
Capital Gains					
Dividends					
Rental Income					
Trust Income					
RETIREMENT INCOME					
Social Security					
Employer's Pension					
Private Pension					
Other					
OTHER INCOME					
Family Contributions					
Gifts					
Unemployment, Disability Insurance					
Alimony/Child Support					
GROSS INCOME	29,000	30,000	500	59,500	4,959

DEDUCTIONS	Husband	Wife	Joint	Total	Monthly
Social Security	2,178	2,253		4,431	369
Federal Taxes	4,500	4,650		9,150	763
State Taxes					
Local Taxes	775	725		1,500	125
Benefits—401(k)					
Other					
TOTAL DEDUCTIONS	7,453	7,628		15,081	1,257
NET INCOME	21,547	22,372	500	44,419	3,702

Worksheet III: The Bucks
SOURCES OF INCOME

EARNED INCOME	Husband	Wife	Joint	Total	Monthly
Wages/Salary	61,000	28,000		89,000	7,417
Self-Employment Income					
Bonus					
INVESTMENT INCOME					
Interest/Savings			1,000	1,000	83
Interest/Bonds					
Capital Gains					
Dividends					
Rental Income					
Trust Income					
RETIREMENT INCOME					
Social Security					
Employer's Pension					
Private Pension					
Other					
OTHER INCOME					
Family Contributions					
Gifts					
Unemployment, Disability Insurance					
Alimony/Child Support					
GROSS INCOME	61,000	28,000	1,000	90,000	7,500

DEDUCTIONS	Husband	Wife	Joint	Total	Monthly
Social Security	3,375	2,253		5,628	469
Federal Taxes	5,600	4,700		10,300	858
State Taxes					
Local Taxes	253			253	21
Benefits—401(k)	6,100			6,100	508
Other					
TOTAL DEDUCTIONS	15,328	6,953		22,281	1,857
NET INCOME	45,672	21,047	1,000	67,719	5,643

Worksheet IV   The McQuarters
FIXED AND FLEXIBLE EXPENSES

SAVINGS	JAN	FEB	MAR	APR	MAY	JUNE	JULY	AUG	SEPT	OCT	NOV	DEC	TOTAL
Emergency													
Short-term Goal													
Other									700				2,800
TOTAL	700			700		700			700				2,800
FIXED EXPENSES													
Rent/Mortgage	320	320	320	320	320	320	320	320	320	320	320	320	3,840
Fuel													0
Electricity	55	60	50	45	52	60	80	110	90	70	55	50	777
Telephone	60	55	60	65	55	40	55	55	60	45	50	50	650
Water	35			40			75			60			210
Homeowner's Insurance		125				0		125					250
Automobile Insurance			125			125			125			125	500
Disability Insurance													0
Medical Insurance	200			200			200			200			800
Life Insurance													0
Life Insurance													0
Life Insurance													0
Personal Property Tax													0
Real Estate Taxes	400						400						800
Automobile Loan	137	137	137	137	137	137	137	137	137	137	137	137	1,644
Loan Repayment													0
Loan Repayment													0
Other Debt													0
Emergency Fund													0
Other													0
TOTAL FIXED EXPENSES	1,207	697	692	807	564	682	1,267	747	732	832	562	682	9,471
Monthly Average	789	789	789	789	789	789	789	789	789	789	789	789	9,468
Difference (Amount to be set aside for fixed expense account)		92	97	107	225	107	42	42	57		227	107	

Worksheet IV: The McQuarters
FIXED AND FLEXIBLE EXPENSES

FLEXIBLE EXPENSES	JAN	FEB	MAR	APR	MAY	JUNE	JULY	AUG	SEPT	OCT	NOV	DEC	TOTAL
Food/Beverage	300	300	300	300	300	300	300	300	300	300	300	300	3,600
Clothing	100		75	80	80	75	50	40	55	60	75	85	775
Laundry/Dry Cleaning													
Home/Office Supplies													
Animals	25		50		35	70		60		70	35	20	365
Personal Care/Toiletries	60			50	20	10	45		35		50	35	305
Periodicals													
Recreation	125			35			125			40			325
Entertainment	25	25	25	45	25	25	25	25	25	25	25	65	360
Travel/Vacation													
Gifts		45	75			50						150	320
HOUSEHOLD MAINTENANCE													
Lawn/Snow Removal													
Maid													
Garbage													
Repairs		50			75			45		10			240
Home Furnishings													
Major Appliances													
TRANSPORTATION													
Gas/Oil	150	150	150	150	150	150	150	150	150	150	150	150	1,800
Repairs		200			85		250						535
Licenses/Registration											75		75
Commutation, Parking													
CHILDREN'S EXPENSES													
Allowances													
Lessons													
Camp													
Babysitting	150	150	150	150	150	150	150	150	150	150	150	150	1,800
Recreation/Sports													

Worksheet IV: The McQuarters
FIXED AND FLEXIBLE EXPENSES

FLEXIBLE EXPENSES	JAN	FEB	MAR	APR	MAY	JUNE	JULY	AUG	SEPT	OCT	NOV	DEC	TOTAL
EDUCATION													
Tuition													
Room/Board													
Books/Supplies													
Travel													
MEDICAL EXPENSES													
Doctor		40		40		40		55		65		55	295
Dentist	35				35			35					105
Drug													
CONTRIBUTIONS													
Church/Synagogue													
Other Charity													
TOTAL SAVINGS	700			700		700			700				2,800
TOTAL FLEXIBLE EXPENSES	970	960	825	850	955	870	1,045	860	715	930	860	1,010	10,900
TOTAL FIXED EXPENSES	1,207	697	692	807	564	682	1,267	747	732	832	562	682	9,471
TOTAL EXPENSES	2,877	1,657	1,517	2,357	1,519	2,252	2,362	1,607	2,147	1,762	1,422	1,692	23,171
NET INCOME													
PROFIT (LOSS)													

BUSINESS EXPENSES	JAN	FEB	MAR	APR	MAY	JUNE	JULY	AUG	SEPT	OCT	NOV	DEC	TOTAL
Instruments/Repairs				500			1,000	75	100	250	35		1,610
Public Relations		45	65		80								555
Office Supplies	40	50		30	25			25	60				230
Music Supplies	35	45		75	80			30		50			315
TOTAL EXPENSES	2,952	1,877	1,582	2,962	1,599	2,357	3,362	1,712	2,307	2,012	1,507	1,692	25,921
INCOME													30,250
PROFIT (LOSS)													4,369

Worksheet IV: The Nicholses
FIXED AND FLEXIBLE EXPENSES

SAVINGS	JAN	FEB	MAR	APR	MAY	JUNE	JULY	AUG	SEPT	OCT	NOV	DEC	TOTAL
Emergency	100	100	100	100	100	100	100	100	100	100	100	100	1,200
Short-term Goal	800	800	800	800	800	800	800	800	800	800	800	800	9,600
Other													
TOTAL	900	900	900	900	900	900	900	900	900	900	900	900	10,800
FIXED EXPENSES													
Rent/Mortgage	925	925	925	925	925	925	925	925	925	925	925	925	11,100
Fuel													
Electricity	58	75	60	65	60	55	75	125	100	60	70	65	868
Telephone	44	35	44	55	35	45	53	56	45	55	35	45	547
Water													
Homeowner's Insurance				100									100
Automobile Insurance	300			300			300			300			1,200
Disability Insurance													
Medical Insurance		125			125			125			125		500
Life Insurance													
Life Insurance													
Life Insurance													
Personal Property Tax													
Real Estate Taxes													
Automobile Loan	257	257	257	257	257	257	257	257	257	257	257	257	3,084
Loan Repayment	206	206	206	206	206	206	206	206	206	206	206	206	2,472
Loan Repayment													
Other Debt	100	100	100	100	100	100	100	100	100	100	100	100	1,200
Emergency Fund													
Other													
TOTAL FIXED EXPENSES	1,890	1,723	1,592	2,008	1,708	1,588	1,916	1,794	1,633	1,903	1,718	1,598	21,071
Monthly Average	1,756	1,756	1,756	1,756	1,756	1,756	1,756	1,756	1,756	1,756	1,756	1,756	
Difference (Amount to be set			164		489	168			123		38	158	
aside for fixed expense													
account)													

Worksheet IV: The Nicholses
FIXED AND FLEXIBLE EXPENSES

FLEXIBLE EXPENSES	JAN	FEB	MAR	APR	MAY	JUNE	JULY	AUG	SEPT	OCT	NOV	DEC	TOTAL
Food/Beverage	200	200	200	200	200	200	200	200	200	200	200	200	2,400
Clothing	150	250			65			275			200	150	1,090
Laundry/Dry Cleaning													
Home/Office Supplies													
Animals	25	15		15		15	150		15		15		250
Personal Care/Toiletries		50			45		50			45			190
Periodicals	20	20	20	20	20	20	20	20	20	20	20	20	240
Recreation													
Entertainment	75	200	75	75	200	75	75	170	75	75	125	75	1,295
Travel/Vacation			1,000										1,000
Gifts		50	35	100			100					200	485
HOUSEHOLD MAINTENANCE													
Lawn/Snow Removal													
Maid													
Garbage													
Repairs													
Home Furnishings													
Major Appliances													
TRANSPORTATION													
Gas/Oil	150	125	150	125	145	110	150	115	120	105	110	103	1,508
Repairs		500		350				250			400		1,500
Licenses/Registration								50				50	100
Commutation, Parking													
CHILDREN'S EXPENSES													
Allowances													
Lessons													
Camp													
Babysitting													
Recreation/Sports													

Worksheet IV: The Nicholses
FIXED AND FLEXIBLE EXPENSES

FLEXIBLE EXPENSES	JAN	FEB	MAR	APR	MAY	JUNE	JULY	AUG	SEPT	OCT	NOV	DEC	TOTAL
EDUCATION													
Tuition													
Room/Board													
Books/Supplies													
Travel													
MEDICAL EXPENSES													
Doctor				65						45			110
Dentist	55					55				55			165
Drug													
CONTRIBUTIONS													
Church/Synagogue													
Other Charity													
TOTAL SAVINGS	900	900	900	900	900	900	900	900	900	900	900	900	10,800
TOTAL FLEXIBLE EXPENSES	675	1,410	1,480	950	675	475	745	1,080	430	545	1,010	798	10,333
TOTAL FIXED EXPENSES	1,890	1,723	1,592	2,008	1,708	1,588	1,916	1,794	1,633	1,903	1,718	1,598	21,071
TOTAL EXPENSES	3,465	4,033	3,972	3,858	3,283	2,963	3,561	3,774	2,963	3,348	3,688	3,096	42,204
NET INCOME													44,419
PROFIT (LOSS)													2,215

FIXED AND FLEXIBLE EXPENSES

SAVINGS	JAN	FEB	MAR	APR	MAY	JUNE	JULY	AUG	SEPT	OCT	NOV	DEC	TOTAL
Emergency													
Short-term Goal													
Other	300	300	300	300	300	300	300	300	300	300	300	300	3,600
TOTAL	300	300	300	300	300	300	300	300	300	300	300	300	3,600
FIXED EXPENSES													
Rent/Mortgage	1,608	1,608	1,608	1,608	1,608	1,608	1,608	1,608	1,608	1,608	1,608	1,608	19,296
Fuel	90	90	90	90	90		90		90	90	90	90	900
Electricity	35	30	50	45	38	60	90	120	85	40	40	35	668
Telephone	75	75	60	65	75	40	50	55	53	48	65	65	726
Water	40			40			125			130			335
Homeowner's Insurance		150				150		150			150		600
Automobile Insurance			135			135			135			135	540
Disability Insurance													
Medical Insurance													
Life Insurance	75	75	75	75	75	75	75	75	75	75	75	75	900
Life Insurance	150			150			150			150			600
Life Insurance													
Personal Property Tax													
Real Estate Taxes	175	175	175	175	175	175	175	175	175	175	175	175	2,100
Automobile Loan	214	214	214	214	214	214	214	214	214	214	214	214	2,568
Loan Repayment	265	265	265	265	265	265	265	265	265	265	265	265	3,180
Loan Repayment													
Other Debt													
Emergency Fund													
Other													
TOTAL FIXED EXPENSES	2,727	2,682	2,672	2,727	2,540	2,722	2,752	2,752	2,700	2,775	2,682	2,662	32,413
Monthly Average	2,701	2,701	2,701	2,701	2,721	2,721	2,701	2,701	2,701	2,701	2,701	2,701	
Difference (Amount to be set aside for fixed expense account)		19	29		161						19	39	

Worksheet IV: The Bucks
FIXED AND FLEXIBLE EXPENSES

FLEXIBLE EXPENSES	JAN	FEB	MAR	APR	MAY	JUNE	JULY	AUG	SEPT	OCT	NOV	DEC	TOTAL
Food/Beverage	600	600	600	600	600	600	600	600	600	600	600	600	7,200
Clothing	450		175	250	375	125	300		400	125	175	150	2,525
Laundry/Dry Cleaning	50	50	50	50	150	50	50	50	125	50	50	100	825
Home/Office Supplies													
Animals	45	35				75							155
Personal Care/Toiletries	60	55	45	150	35	45	100	554	75	50	50	125	1,344
Periodicals	25	25	45	25	25	55	25	25	65	25	25	125	490
Recreation		100					125			400			625
Entertainment	75	85	125	110	75	75	60	75	60	160	135	200	1,235
Travel/Vacation							500						500
Gifts			150				350			75		500	1,075
HOUSEHOLD MAINTENANCE													
Lawn/Snow Removal	25		35		75		75			150			360
Maid		75						75					150
Garbage	15	15	15	15	15	15	15	15	15	15	15	15	180
Repairs		50			75			45		70			240
Home Furnishings		150		75				225					450
Major Appliances													
TRANSPORTATION													
Gas/Oil	130	130	130	130	130	130	130	130	130	130	130	130	1,560
Repairs			300			165			75				540
Licenses/Registration											75		75
Commutation, Parking													
CHILDREN'S EXPENSES													
Allowances													
Lessons													
Camp						500							500
Babysitting	850	850	850	850	850	850	850	850	850	850	850	850	10,200
Recreation/Sports													

Worksheet IV: The Bucks
FIXED AND FLEXIBLE EXPENSES

FLEXIBLE EXPENSES	JAN	FEB	MAR	APR	MAY	JUNE	JULY	AUG	SEPT	OCT	NOV	DEC	TOTAL
EDUCATION													
Tuition													
Room/Board													
Books/Supplies													
Travel													
MEDICAL EXPENSES													
Doctor													
Dentist													
Drug													
CONTRIBUTIONS													
Church/Synagogue	50	50	50	50	50	50	50	50	50	50	50	50	600
Other Charity													
TOTAL SAVINGS	300	300	300	300	300	300	300	300	300	300	300	300	3,600
TOTAL FLEXIBLE EXPENSES	2,450	2,195	2,570	2,305	2,455	2,735	3,230	2,694	2,445	2,750	2,155	2,845	30,829
TOTAL FIXED EXPENSES	2,727	2,682	2,672	2,727	2,546	2,722	2,752	2,752	2,700	2,795	2,682	2,662	32,413
TOTAL EXPENSES	5,477	5,177	5,542	5,332	5,295	5,757	6,282	5,746	5,445	5,845	5,137	5,807	66,842
NET INCOME													66,719
PROFIT (LOSS)													547

Worksheet III: Yours
SOURCES OF INCOME

EARNED INCOME	Husband	Wife	Joint	Total	Monthly
Wages/Salary					
Self-Employment Income					
Bonus					
INVESTMENT INCOME					
Interest/Savings					
Interest/Bonds					
Capital Gains					
Dividends					
Rental Income					
Trust Income					
RETIREMENT INCOME					
Social Security					
Employer's Pension					
Private Pension					
Other					
OTHER INCOME					
Family Contributions					
Gifts					
Unemployment, Disability Insurance					
Alimony/Child Support					
GROSS INCOME					

DEDUCTIONS	Husband	Wife	Joint	Total	Monthly
Social Security					
Federal Taxes					
State Taxes					
Local Taxes					
Benefits—401(k)					
Other					
TOTAL DEDUCTIONS					
NET INCOME					

Worksheet IV: Yours
FIXED AND FLEXIBLE EXPENSES

	JAN	FEB	MAR	APR	MAY	JUNE	JULY	AUG	SEPT	OCT	NOV	DEC	TOTAL
SAVINGS													
Emergency													
Short-term Goal													
Other													
TOTAL													
FIXED EXPENSES													
Rent/Mortgage													
Fuel													
Electricity													
Telephone													
Water													
Homeowner's Insurance													
Automobile Insurance													
Disability Insurance													
Medical Insurance													
Life Insurance													
Life Insurance													
Life Insurance													
Personal Property Tax													
Real Estate Taxes													
Automobile Loan													
Loan Repayment													
Loan Repayment													
Other Debt													
Emergency Fund													
Other													
TOTAL FIXED EXPENSES													
Monthly Average													
Difference (Amount to be set aside for fixed expense account)													

Worksheet IV: Yours
FIXED AND FLEXIBLE EXPENSES

FLEXIBLE EXPENSES	JAN	FEB	MAR	APR	MAY	JUNE	JULY	AUG	SEPT	OCT	NOV	DEC	TOTAL
Food/Beverage													
Clothing													
Laundry/Dry Cleaning													
Home/Office Supplies													
Animals													
Personal Care/Toiletries													
Periodicals													
Recreation													
Entertainment													
Travel/Vacation													
Gifts													
HOUSEHOLD MAINTENANCE													
Lawn/Snow Removal													
Maid													
Garbage													
Repairs													
Home Furnishings													
Major Appliances													
TRANSPORTATION													
Gas/Oil													
Repairs													
Licenses/Registration													
Commutation, Parking													
CHILDREN'S EXPENSES													
Allowances													
Lessons													
Camp													
Babysitting													
Recreation/Sports													

Worksheet IV: Yours
FIXED AND FLEXIBLE EXPENSES

FLEXIBLE EXPENSES	JAN	FEB	MAR	APR	MAY	JUNE	JULY	AUG	SEPT	OCT	NOV	DEC	TOTAL
EDUCATION													
Tuition													
Room/Board													
Books/Supplies													
Travel													
MEDICAL EXPENSES													
Doctor													
Dentist													
Drug													
CONTRIBUTIONS													
Church/Synagogue													
Other Charity													
TOTAL SAVINGS													
TOTAL FLEXIBLE EXPENSES													
TOTAL FIXED EXPENSES													
TOTAL EXPENSES													
NET INCOME													
PROFIT (LOSS)													

THE BAROMETER OF FINANCIAL FITNESS: YOUR NET WORTH

7

Before you can begin to plan anything, you've got to know just where you stand—right now. And then as you move along in the future, you will need to know where you are financially.

This chapter is to help you see where you are now and to show you how to keep track of where you are over all the years of your marriage and financial partnership.

The two key words are: *net worth*. They sound like something bookkeepers and accountants talk about when they figure out how a business stands. They also make up a phrase that life insurance salespeople use when they are analyzing what kind of coverage they recommend.

Why is it important to know your net worth? Let me answer that by explaining exactly what your net worth is. It is the difference between your assets and your liabilities or debts: the difference between all the money and tangibles that you possess and all the unpaid bills, out-

standing loans, taxes and other obligations you may have. You'll get descriptive details on all that in this chapter. But the basic point I want to make, up front, is that if you don't know your net worth you haven't got a marriage or financial partnership.

So what you've both got to figure out is: Just what is our net worth? What is the difference between what we have and what we owe?

You can do this as individuals or as a couple—or both ways. For the purposes of this chapter, let's consider your net worth as a couple.

Some tough questions

Ask yourselves questions like these:

• Are we saving any money? Are our savings growing?

- Have we started making any investments? Are *they* growing?
- Are our investments producing income?
- Are we in debt? How much? Too much?
- Are we keeping up with inflation? Or ahead of it?

You cannot answer such questions unless you know your net worth. It is the basis for any sound strategy for savings and investment, especially for your children's education. And in the years ahead it will be the basis for your retirement planning and estate planning—two subjects that may seem far in the future but that you will want to start thinking about before too long.

Knowing your net worth at any time can give you real security both now and in the future. Why? Because, if it shows positive signs, you know you have a realistic basis on which to make financial decisions about investments, home buying, raising a family. And if it shows negative signs, you know where you must reduce debt, change investments, or hold off on decisions that cost money.

As I said, your net worth is the difference between your assets and your liabilities, or debts. Let's talk first about assets.

What are all your "pluses"?

Turn to Worksheet VI on page 66. As accurately as you can, write down the actual value of all your assets—money in checking accounts, savings accounts, money market funds; or such securities as stocks, bonds or mutual funds.

> *Note:* Except for regular checking accounts, these are all *income–producing assets.* They pay you *interest* or *dividends* on a regular periodic basis (usually quarterly), and a fixed rate of percentage.

Next, write down the value of any real estate you own. This should be the current market value if you were to sell it today. Put down the cash value of any whole life insurance policies (see Chapter 11) you have (not the "face value" that the policy would pay in case of death, but the amount you would get back if you simply turned in the policy today and stopped paying for it; this is shown in a table in the policy

itself). And add any other long–term assets, as shown on the worksheet.

Personal property comes next. This is the value of your car, furniture, clothing, jewelry, collections, whatever.

> *Note:* These are *non–income–producing assets.* Unlike savings or investments, they just sit there. But, it is to be hoped, some—such as silver or precious gems (diamonds, for example), or collections (books or stamps, maybe)—will increase in real value as time goes by. They are *appreciating.*

Some thoughts about assets

- *Income* is a key word when you talk about assets. Always be sure you know whether an asset is going to produce income and, if so, how much. If it is definitely a non–income–producing asset, be aware of whether it does, nevertheless, appreciate over time. Some boats, for instance, actually appreciate. Most automobiles do not. Houses usually do, as does most real estate.
- *Needs* change. What you are doing at various stages of life will dictate what you want your assets to do for you. At times your income from wages or salary will be all you need. But when your children hit college age, or when you retire, income from assets will be very important. Assets have to be evaluated as needs and circumstances change.
- *Insurance* is a bargain when you're young. See Chapter 11 for details on insurance, but let's say here and now that if you buy insurance at a young age you not only buy protection against bad news but you start to build up cash surrender values that will be important future assets. Some parents have paid for entire college educations by borrowing on cash surrender values in insurance policies they bought when the college students were babes in arms.
- *Income–producing assets* may not be your thing right now. Probably you are both working and producing two salaries, but chances are you find it important to spend what you can on non–income–producing assets for the time being—until you have the home and furnishings you want, for instance, or until you've got the car or have done the

traveling that you had planned. But do think about the insurance, because those rates go up just as regularly as your birthdays come around.

- *Planning* is vital. Think and talk together about what assets you want and what you want them to give you—your home, those college educations.
- *Assets are not set in concrete.* There's no law against selling off certain assets. You don't have to stay in the same house, hold onto the same collectibles, stick with the same securities. If assets are large, your insurance, retirement insurance, and retirement assets can be smaller. If all other assets are small, your insurance and retirement accounts should be larger. Since no two couples are in quite the same boat, you have to analyze your own situation and make your own decision.
- *How much are things worth?* A dealer or appraiser can tell you the current value of a car, a diamond, a rare stamp, an antique doll. A reputable specialized magazine may include listings you can depend on. Your daily newspaper will tell you today's market value of stocks, bonds, and mutual funds. A reliable real estate broker can give you a pretty good fix on the value of your home, if you already own one. And check your local paper for ads giving prices for comparable houses.

How much do you owe?

Now for the liabilities. Start with current bills. List everything you have been billed for but have not yet paid—as of today. Put down any taxes that are unpaid, including all that have not been deducted from your paycheck (federal or state income tax), any capital gains tax, real estate taxes, personal property taxes on a car or boat.

If you now own a house or condominium or vacation home, write down the unpaid balance on the mortgage. What about installment debt? Whatever you currently owe to MasterCard, VISA, or other rotating charge accounts should be listed. Add the unpaid balances on loans for a car, home improvement, education, or life insurance, or other personal loans.

Check and double–check. Make sure you have listed every asset and every liability that exists in your lives.

Now total each column—assets and liabilities. Subtract the liabilities from the assets. The result is your net worth as of today.

Note: If your liabilities turn out to be greater than your assets, you have a "negative net worth"—a precarious situation that should command your immediate attention.

Repeat—how often?

You can't go back and redo your Net Worth Statement weekly or even monthly to reflect the fluctuations that are bound to occur. But you should remember to revise it whenever your major needs and situations change. When you buy a new car, sign for a mortgage on a house or condo, inherit securities, become vested in an employee profit–sharing plan, put savings into an IRA or 401(k), you should dust off the Net Worth Statement and see how it all stacks up under the new conditions.

By all means, review it at least once a year. It is indeed the barometer of your financial situation. Before you make any major decision, a look at your Net Worth Statement can give you a sound basis for figuring out which way to go.

THE McQUARTERS' NET WORTH...

With every nail that is hammered into their house, Valerie and James see the value of their home go up. "When we have the money, we start fixing up another room, add some landscaping or repair what needs to be done," says James. "Sometimes, I wish we could finish it all at once. But, at the same time, it's exciting doing one step at a time." They financed the house with the previous owners, and they still owe a small amount on a car loan.

...AND THE BUCKS'...

Over their eight–year marriage, the Bucks have managed to save. In fact, saving was easier before their last move. And they do have a money–market

Worksheet V: The McQuarters
NET WORTH STATEMENT

ASSETS	Self	Spouse	Joint	Total
CURRENT ASSETS				
Cash on Hand				
Checking Account			500	500
Savings Account			2,500	2,500
Credit Union Accounts				
Money Market Accounts				
Certificates of Deposit				
Treasury Bills				
Savings Bonds				
Other				
Sub Total			3,000	3,000
INVESTMENTS				
Stocks				
Bonds				
Tax Exempt Bonds				
Mutual Funds				
Government Securities				
Tax Shelters				
Investment Club				
Other				
Sub Total				
REAL ESTATE				
Personal Residence			50,000	50,000
Recreational Property				
Income Property				
Sub Total			50,000	50,000
LONG-TERM ASSETS				
Cash Value Life Insurance				
Annuities				
Individual Retirement Accounts				
Keogh Plans				
Pension Plan				
Profit Sharing Plan				
Business Interest				
Other				
Sub Total				
PERSONAL PROPERTY				
Home Furnishings			1,000	1,000
Clothing and Furs				

ASSETS	Self	Spouse	Joint	Total
Jewelry				
Automobiles				
Antiques				
Stamp Collection				
Coins				
Fine Art				
Other—Musical Equipment			10,000	10,000
Sub Total			11,000	11,000
TOTAL			64,000	64,000

LIABILITIES	Self	Spouse	Joint	Total
CURRENT LIABILITIES				
Medical and Dental				
Current Bills			750	750
Charge Accounts				
Sub Total			750	750
UNPAID TAXES				
Federal			1,400	1,400
State				
Local				
Sub Total			1,400	1,400
REAL ESTATE				
Residence			21,000	21,000
Recreational				
Income Property				
Sub Total			21,000	21,000
OTHER INSTALLMENT DEBT				
Automobile Loans			1,500	1,500
Home Improvement Loans				
Education Loans				
Life Insurance Loans				
Margin Accounts				
Bank Loans				
Credit Cards				
Other			1,000	1,000
Sub Total			2,500	2,500
TOTAL			25,650	25,650
TOTAL ASSETS			64,000	64,000
TOTAL LIABILITIES			25,650	25,650
NET WORTH			38,350	38,350

account for emergencies. "The house has gone up in value, but we have a huge mortgage on it," says Pat. "And we have the two car loans. There's no question that the pre-tax savings plan at work has helped us to save. Also, we saved in Individual Retirement Accounts for several years."

There are many questions that come up when you start evaluating whether your assets meet the Financial Fitness test. Now that you have analyzed your lifestyle and worked out your priorities from your budgeting process, you should begin to consider your assets.

When, or how often, should you evaluate assets? The answer is, every couple of years at least, and more often if you have any major changes in lifestyle, family situation (such as children who have left the nest), or in the assets themselves.

A good reason for not evaluating your assets until now is the fact that assets usually cost you something—unless you inherit them—and it's important to work out your budget first.

Income is the key word when you talk about assets. Some assets produce income. Some do not. Always the hope is that assets that are not producing income right now will keep quietly growing until the day you sell or liquidate them. One hopes they are *appreciating*.

Different needs at various stages of your life dictate what you want assets to do for you. There are times when income from wages or salary is adequate—and times when it is not. When your children are in college or when you are in retirement, income from salary or from a pension may not be enough. Income from assets will then be extremely valuable.

View assets three ways

When you look at assets, you need three viewpoints: one of your assets, one of your insurance plans, one of your retirement program. If assets are large, insurance plans and retirement programs can be smaller. If assets are small, insurance and retirement programs should be larger. No two cases are alike, so you have to size up all the angles.

If you are like most young couples or young singles, the chances are you have no income-producing assets. The two of you are working, producing two salaries, and spending as much as you can on non-income-producing assets such as furniture, house, or collectibles. So this is the time to buy insurance, while young rates apply, and let cash values start to build up—they will be future assets.

When a young couple makes the commitment to buy their first home, their net worth picture changes dramatically. From this point on, they add to personal possessions with furniture and other household possessions, often without keeping a tight rein on credit. Yet this is the very time when planning should be made for assets that will pay for college expenses in 15 or 20 years.

With income increasing as the family grows in age, size, and number, insurance and its cash values should be looked at every few years. Investments should be watched more closely and bought for growth when the children are young, then realigned to produce more income as the college years approach.

Few people can pay college expenses out of salary. But if you have built up income-producing assets over the years, they can help meet this gigantic expenditure. And, before you start borrowing at high interest rates to pay for college, you may be pleasantly surprised by what you have built up over those 15 or 20 years.

When the kids move out

The empty-nest period brings another change. The years between the end of the children's education and retirement is the time to invest again for growth and appreciation and to make plans for the retirement years. If Mom returns to the work force, two incomes can now help build up the assets, especially with expenses dropping as the children move out on their own. (Surprise! Even the electricity bill drops a little when daughters no longer run hair dryers and stereos are not turned on 24 hours a day.) At this point, salaries should once again pay living expenses and leave some extra to build up assets.

The idea now will be to invest for capital appreciation that can be converted into actual income during the retirement years. Credit obligations should be avoided or kept to a minimum.

Worksheet V: The Bucks
NET WORTH STATEMENT

ASSETS	Self	Spouse	Joint	Total
CURRENT ASSETS				
Cash on Hand				
Checking Account	500	650	750	1,900
Savings Account				
Credit Union Accounts				
Money Market Accounts			8,500	8,500
Certificates of Deposit				
Treasury Bills				
Savings Bonds				
Other				
Sub Total	500	650	9,250	10,400
INVESTMENTS				
Stocks				
Bonds				
Tax Exempt Bonds				
Mutual Funds				
Government Securities				
Tax Shelters				
Investment Club				
Other				
Sub Total				
REAL ESTATE				
Personal Residence			262,000	262,000
Recreational Property				
Income Property				
Sub Total			262,000	262,000
LONG-TERM ASSETS				
Cash Value Life Insurance				
Annuities				
Individual Retirement Accounts	12,000	5,000		17,000
401(k) Plans				
Keogh Plans				
Pension Plans				
Profit Sharing Plans				
Business Interest				
Other	63,500			63,500
Sub Total	75,500	5,000		80,500

ASSETS	Self	Spouse	Joint	Total
PERSONAL PROPERTY				
Home Furnishings			7,500	7,500
Clothing and Furs				
Jewelry				
Automobiles	10,000		12,000	22,000
Antiques				
Stamp Collection				
Coins				
Fine Art				
Other—Musical Equipment				
Sub Total	10,000		19,500	29,500
TOTAL	86,000	5,650	290,750	382,400

LIABILITIES	Self	Spouse	Joint	Total
CURRENT LIABILITIES				
Medical and Dental				
Current Bills				
Charge Accounts		450	1,000	1,450
Sub Total		450	1,000	1,450
UNPAID TAXES				
Federal				
State				
Local				
Sub Total				
REAL ESTATE				
Residence			198,000	198,000
Recreational				
Income Property				
Sub Total			198,000	198,000
OTHER INSTALLMENT DEBT				
Automobile Loans			18,500	18,500
Home Improvement Loans				
Education Loans				
Life Insurance Loans				
Margin Accounts				
Bank Loans				
Credit Cards			3,000	3,000
Other				
Sub Total			21,500	21,500
TOTAL		450	220,500	220,950
TOTAL ASSETS	86,000	5,650	290,750	382,400
TOTAL LIABILITIES		450	220,500	220,950
NET WORTH	86,000	5,200	70,250	161,450

ASSETS	Self	Spouse	Joint	Total
CURRENT ASSETS				
Cash on Hand				
Checking Account				
Savings Account				
Credit Union Accounts				
Money Market Accounts				
Certificates of Deposit				
Treasury Bills				
Savings Bonds				
Other				
Sub Total				
INVESTMENTS				
Stocks				
Bonds				
Tax Exempt Bonds				
Mutual Funds				
Government Securities				
Tax Shelters				
Investment Club				
Other				
Sub Total				
REAL ESTATE				
Personal Residence				
Recreational Property				
Income Property				
Sub Total				
LONG-TERM ASSETS				
Cash Value Life Insurance				
Annuities				
Individual Retirement Accounts				
401(k) Plans				
Keogh Plans				
Pension Plans				
Profit Sharing Plans				
Business Interest				
Other				
Sub Total				

ASSETS	Self	Spouse	Joint	Total
PERSONAL PROPERTY				
Home Furnishings	___	___	___	___
Clothing and Furs	___	___	___	___
Jewelry	___	___	___	___
Automobiles	___	___	___	___
Antiques	___	___	___	___
Stamp Collection	___	___	___	___
Coins	___	___	___	___
Fine Art	___	___	___	___
Other—Musical Equipment	___	___	___	___
Sub Total	___	___	___	___
TOTAL	___	___	___	___

LIABILITIES	Self	Spouse	Joint	Total
CURRENT LIABILITIES				
Medical and Dental	___	___	___	___
Current Bills	___	___	___	___
Charge Accounts	___	___	___	___
Sub Total	___	___	___	___
UNPAID TAXES				
Federal	___	___	___	___
State	___	___	___	___
Local	___	___	___	___
Sub Total	___	___	___	___
REAL ESTATE				
Residence	___	___	___	___
Recreational	___	___	___	___
Income Property	___	___	___	___
Sub Total	___	___	___	___
OTHER INSTALLMENT DEBT				
Automobile Loans	___	___	___	___
Home Improvement Loans	___	___	___	___
Education Loans	___	___	___	___
Life Insurance Loans	___	___	___	___
Margin Accounts	___	___	___	___
Bank Loans	___	___	___	___
Credit Cards	___	___	___	___
Other	___	___	___	___
Sub Total	___	___	___	___
TOTAL	___	___	___	___
TOTAL ASSETS	___	___	___	___
TOTAL LIABILITIES	___	___	___	___
NET WORTH	___	___	___	___

Now your Net Worth Statement will tell you what your assets are, and your Budget sheets will tell the cost of maintaining them.

There is never any real harm in selling off certain assets. You earned the money to buy them in the first place. You are not stuck with them forever. Must you stay in the same house, for instance, even if it has empty rooms? Now that your children are earning their own way, do you really need the same high insurance coverage you bought when they were in grade school? You have a number of options at this point.

Use the **Asset Evaluation Worksheet** to size up your income–producing and non–income–producing assets.

Income–producing assets

Pick up current assets (checking and savings accounts, securities, and so on) from your Net Worth Statement. (See page 63.) Note that except for broker's fees or commissions, these cost you nothing to own or maintain. Fill in annual income from the "sources of income" section of your Budget sheet; yields should come from your Record–keeping sheets.

Non–income–producing assets

Fill in your real estate, personal property, and other long–term assets here. Don't forget such items as fine art and coin and stamp collections. In this area you do have annual costs of ownership: taxes, utilities, and maintenance on the house; premium payments on insurance; insurance premiums on personal property such as a car or boat. The costs of owning these assets come from your fixed expenses budget.

Net sale value is the amount you would get if you sold a particular asset; the market value of your house, for example, minus such costs of selling as real estate commission, legal fees, and so on. There may also be a fee when you sell collectibles.

Worksheet VI: Yours ASSETS EVALUATION				
INCOME-PRODUCING ASSETS **Current Assets**	**NET SALE VALUE**	**ANNUAL INCOME** (From Budget)	**% YIELD** (Income ÷ Market Value)	**ANNUAL COST OF OWNERSHIP** (From Budget)
Checking Accounts				
Savings Accounts				
Credit Union Accounts				
Money Market Funds				
Certificates of Deposit				
Treasury Bills				
Treasury Notes				
Securities				
Stocks				
Bonds				
Mutual Funds				
Total				

Worksheet VI: Yours
ASSETS EVALUATION

INCOME-PRODUCING ASSETS Current Assets	NET SALE VALUE	ANNUAL INCOME (From Budget)	% YIELD (Income ÷ Market Value)	ANNUAL COST OF OWNERSHIP (From Budget)
NON-INCOME-PRODUCING				
Personal Residence				
Recreational Property				
Cash Value Life Insurance				
Business Interests				
Home Furnishings				
Automobiles				
Jewelry				
Antiques—Fine Art				
Coin Collection				
Stamp Collection				
Total				

DEBT: HOW TO GET INTO IT, AND OUT AGAIN— WITHOUT GETTING HURT

8

You're settled into the condominium. You went for it all—the deep plush carpet that was *so* better looking (and feeling!) than that standard, looks–like–an–office–or–a–mall carpet that came with the deal...the Renaissance floor tile in the kitchen and entry...the deluxe bathroom, with its Jacuzzi tub and built–in sauna...the sconces with the special little candle–flame bulbs over the fireplace.

And you've added the rear–projection TV, the top–of–the–line compact disc player, the state–of–the–art VCR. And that's not to mention the new microwave–convection oven that makes all other microwaves obsolete.

Now you're thinking about the BMW.

"Well, I do pick up clients. For meetings with some of our suppliers. Or to go to lunch. I can justify it."

"But we've got the Honda. And the Bronco II."

"So we'll trade the Honda. Keep the Bronco II. Gotta have that for the weekends. And we ought to put oversize tires on it so we can go for those blues at the shore."

And so it goes.

And then one day you realize it. The Bronco II and the beautiful new BMW (bought on a not–too–bad deal for the Honda), combined with several other big–ticket items, have rolled you right into a trap. It's an easy trap to fall into—the trap of over–extended credit—because the world has been on a spending spree throughout your lifetimes. At least, the world you and I know has—the world of the U.S. dollar. Credit has been easy to get. Anyone who wants to buy now and pay later has been welcome to do so, and in fact everyone has been encouraged to do just that. I won't bore you with a litany of the instant gratifications of desires that we have all become used to. It's a world in which you can have what you want when you want it and somehow find a way to pay the price.

Credit is nothing new. Debt goes back hundreds of years. Shakespeare talked of borrowers and lenders. Dickens saw Mr. Micawber in and out of debtors' prison. But *consumer* credit as a system of borrowing and repaying really began in this country in 1856 when Isaac Singer hit upon the idea of time payments—$5 down and $5 a month—to sell his $125 sewing machines at a time when the average American's annual income was $525.

Singer's system generated sales that never could have been achieved if people had had to pay cash. Over the years, buying big–ticket items "on time" and paying for them while you used them became standard for millions of Americans. It also created a vast industry that includes bank loan departments, credit unions, General Motors Acceptance Corporation, loan sharks, and countless others.

For the purposes of this chapter, by the way, credit means credit as handled by such organizations as I've just mentioned. I'm *not* talking about home mortgages.

All–purpose credit cards are a more recent phenomenon. Diner's Club started it all, in 1950. The total outstanding debt of American consumers then stood at $21.5 billion. Thirty years later—with American Express, VISA, MasterCard and many others in line with Diner's Club—the figure had reached over $600 billion.

Renting money

What is credit? It is a means of renting money when you need it and for as long as you need it. It is just as practical as renting a car or a U-Haul trailer or a chain saw. Rental firms charge a rental fee; credit firms charge you interest. When interest rates rise, you pay the lender more for the money you borrow, just as you would pay more for the trailer or chain saw if the rental company raised its rates.

There are two basic types of consumer credit:

1. *Open–ended or "revolving" credit.* This is the type you can use over and over again, usually up to a certain borrowing limit that is arranged in advance. It includes such credit cards as VISA, MasterCard and Diner's Club; department store charge cards; and cash reserve on your checking account. ***Note:*** VISA and MasterCard, and perhaps some others, have a way of sending you a notice, after you have proved that you are a dependable repayer, informing you that because you are so good they have increased the amount you are permitted to charge at any one time. Be wary of this trap. Make your own decisions about what your limits are.

2. *Installment loan credit.* Here you borrow a specific amount for a specific purpose and pay it back over a specific period, with due dates agreed upon. This type of loan is used for big–ticket items: automobiles, boats, mobile homes or recreation vehicles, home improvements.

Where can you borrow?

- *Small loan companies.* Also known as consumer finance companies, these specialize in loans with limits ranging from a few hundred dollars to thousands of dollars. These companies will make loans for almost any conceivable purpose,

- *Credit unions.* These are "co–ops." Usually tied into a labor union at the place where you work, they make loans to their members (all borrowers must be shareholders in the credit union) for any reasonable purpose. Greatest advantage: The credit union rate of interest is usually lower than that of other financial institutions.

- *Commercial banks.* Traditionally, their credit customers were businesspeople and farmers. In the past 30 years, however, they have moved into the area of personal loans in a big way, showing more rapid growth than any other type of lending institution.

- *Savings and loan associations.* While their business is mainly making mortgage loans out of the capital they amass from savings deposits, they are permitted, in many states, to make consumer loans as well. Compare your local S & Ls versus commercial banks and savings banks.

- *Life insurance companies.* If you are buying life insurance that builds up savings, you can borrow the cash value from the insurance company or use the policy as security on a loan from a bank. (See

Chapter 11 on insurance.) Usually after a policy has been in force for a few years, it has built up a cash value, and you can either surrender the policy and accept a lump sum in cash, or borrow out a specific amount and keep the policy in force.

Secured versus unsecured loans

If your loan is "secured," it means you must pledge something of value as collateral—an automobile, a savings account, or some other personal property—which the lender is legally entitled to take away from you if you do not repay the loan. An "unsecured" loan demands no collateral. You pay a higher rate of interest for an unsecured loan.

What does credit cost?

Prices vary. But whatever the cost, the creditor must tell you, under the Truth in Lending Law—in writing and before you sign any agreement—exactly what is the annual percentage rate (APR) and just how much the total finance charge will be for the period over which you are borrowing the money.

The *finance charge* is the total *dollar* amount you may pay in order to use credit. It can include not only the cost of interest but service charges, and some credit–related premiums, such as credit life insurance or appraisal fees.

The *annual percentage rate (APR)* is the relative cost of credit on a yearly basis, expressed as a *percentage* reflecting all costs of your loan. It is the key to comparing costs between one lender and another. Figuring their APRs involves complex mathematical computations, but all lenders have tables that do the work. In essence, let me describe the situation this way: If you borrow $1,000 from me for a year at 10 percent, you'll pay me back $1,000 plus interest a year later. But if you go to a bank and borrow the $1,000 you will repay it in 12 equal monthly installments that include the interest. This means you won't really have the use of the entire $1,000 for the entire year. In effect, you'll get to use less and less of it each month, and the APR will be more than a simple 10 percent.

Note: Interest limits are set by state governments. Some permit higher limits than others.

The finance charges on credit cards such as VISA and MasterCard are set by the bank that issues the card, not by the card company. So a bank offering VISA in Connecticut, for instance, may set its finance charge only as high as 18 percent, while a bank in South Dakota may charge its VISA customers up to 25 percent.

How do you get credit?

If you have never borrowed money or bought anything on credit, how do you "get credit" in the first place?

The situation is a Catch–22. You cannot get credit until you prove you can be depended on to pay your debts, and you cannot get debts to pay until someone takes the risk of extending credit to you.

If you are applying for your first credit card—either singly or for a joint card—you may have a tough time at first. A lender will ask you to fill out an application form. The creditor is looking for three things:

1. Do you have the capability of repaying? What is your present income from all sources—including dividends on investments or part–time employment?
2. What are your assets?
3. Do you have the willingness to pay? If you have no previous history of repayments, this is the Catch–22. For example, when my daughter first applied for a credit card in her own name, she didn't have enough income to qualify for the card, so I was asked to be a cosigner for her. This meant that my income and credit history were used to enable her to qualify, and I was as liable for payments on her account as she was. Yet the card was in her name and was reported to credit bureaus as such, so that she began to establish a credit identity of her own.

What can you do, if you are refused credit on your own the first time you apply—and if you cannot find a cosigner? Try these suggestions:

- Insist on finding out which credit bureau has reported on you and how accurate they are. Recently the Federal Trade Commission reported that one of the nation's largest bureaus, the Trans Union Credit Information Company, had been making a "significant" number of errors in its reports on consumers. Mix–ups included sending a file with the correct name but the wrong address, ZIP code, or Social Security number to credit granters.

- Open checking and savings accounts at a local bank in your own name. Get to know your banker.
- When you have a savings account established, borrow against it. A savings account shows you are in the habit of saving. A bank that is considering your application for a personal loan, for instance, should look favorably on this, and would use the balance in your savings account as security. This would mean, of course, that you could not withdraw from your savings the amount the bank considered security until the loan was repaid.
- Apply for a charge account at a local store. Pay it promptly each month.
- Establish an installment loan at a local store, purchasing something on the layaway plan rather than simply charging.
- Apply for a small bank loan—even if you don't need it. Put the money in a savings account. Withdraw enough each month to make the payments on the loan.
- Try obtaining a credit card (VISA or MasterCard) through the bank where you have established your checking account and where the banker now knows you and knows you are OK.

How the lender views it

Whether it is a bank, a store, American Express, Diner's Club—whatever the firm—it is taking a chance on *you*, based on *your* current income and circumstances, when it agrees to let you have credit. So the creditor has the right to know whether or not you are a good risk—whether you have a savings account and/or a checking account, whether you rent your living space or own it, how long you have been at that location, how long you've worked for the same employer. From all this information, the lender decides how much of a chance he or she is taking on you.

WHEN ERIC NICHOLS APPLIED FOR HIS FIRST MASTERCARD...

...he was told he would have to have a cosigner. "I had no credit history," says Eric, "and my income was minimal. My mom co–signed and told me in no uncertain terms that she would cancel if she found out I hadn't paid the bill promptly every month. You better believe I paid it in full each month. And finally—after I proved I was reliable over about a year's time, I got another card in my own name without a cosigner." By the time he needed a car loan to buy his RV, Eric had a steady income and a good credit history. Today, Jeanne and Eric are careful to charge only what they can pay each month. They treat their credit cards as strictly convenience.

Your credit record

Once you have acquired credit, remember that it is an obligation that you have agreed to pay back. Never abuse it. List this monthly obligation as a fixed expense on your budget sheet, and repay it just as you pay your rent, utilities, and other fixed expenses.

Now you are building up your credit record. Next time you seek credit, the lender will be able to obtain a "credit report" on you from a *credit bureau*—any one of some 2,000 firms in the United States that act as clearinghouses for information about consumers' debts and bill–paying habits. Banks, finance companies, stores, and other creditors feed information about their customers into these credit bureaus.

Should you worry about your credit profile? Not unless you are refused credit for no apparent reason, or unless you have failed to keep up with payments and are in trouble with some account somewhere.

Some things you should know about credit bureaus:

- They do not assign credit ratings or make judgments on your ability to repay. They simply sell creditors a look at your profile, which then speaks for itself. It is the bank, store, gasoline company,

Exhibit 6 page 1

TRW CREDIT DATA — UPDATED CREDIT PROFILE — CONFIDENTIAL

INQUIRY INFORMATION

TCR2

DFD2 9999999ABC
S-548926847, 987 MAIN ST BIG CITY, NY 10001

PAGE	DATE	TIME	PORT	HV	CONSUMER		02-999999/99
1	08-01-90	15:19:14	AL11	A14			

John Consumer
987 Main
Big City, NY 10001

A & B ACC'T
460 S. PARK
BIG CITY, NY 10001

SS# 044-56-0334

YOB 1956

ACCOUNT PROFILE			SUBSCRIBER NAME/COURT NAME			SUBSCRIBER # COURT CODE	ASSN CODE	AMOUNT	BALANCE	ACCOUNT NUMBER/DOCKET		PAYMENT PROFILE NUMBER OF MONTHS PRIOR TO BALANCE DATE
POS	NON	NEG	STATUS COMMENT	DATE REPORTED INQUIRY	DATE OPENED	TYPE	TERMS	AMOUNT	BALANCE	BALANCE DATE	AMOUNT PAST DUE	1 2 3 4 5 6 7 8 9 10 11 12
A			NATIONAL BANK CURR	6/15/90	7/88	AUT	2 48	$7,000	$4,000	402245 7/1/90		CCCCCCCCCCCC
	M		DECORATOR'S FURN CURR WAS 30-3	6/15/90	1/88	CHG	2 60	$5,000	$3,000	892941 7/15/90	$75	C1CC1CC11CC1
		A	VISA CURR 60 PAS		9/87	CHG	2 REV	$2,000	$1,200	32214 6/20/90	$70	CCC11CCCC1C1
		A	MASTER CURR 60 PAS		7/87	CHG	2 REV	$2,500	$1,500	41221 6/30/90	$100	1CCC1CC1CC11
A			BLOOMING-DALE'S CURR ACT		10/87	CHG	2 REV	$1,500	$1,100	12211 7/10/90		CCCCCCCCCC1C

© TRW INC. 1971, 1978

Exhibit 6 page 2

NAME OF CREDIT GRANTOR — TO THE ATTENTION OF

SIGNATURE ______ DATE ______

EXPLANATION OF INFORMATION ON FORM

TRW *CREDIT DATA* — *UPDATED CREDIT PROFILE* — *CONFIDENTIAL*

1 INQUIRY INFORMATION

PAGE	DATE	TIME	PORT	H V

2

ACCOUNT PROFILE 3			SUBSCRIBER NAME COURT NAME 4			SUBSCRIBER # COURT CODE 5	ASSN CODE 6	AMOUNT		ACCOUNT DOCKET NUMBER 7		PAYMENT PROFILE MONTHS PRIOR TO BALANCE DATE 17
POS	NON	NEG	STATUS COMMENTS 8	DATE REPORTED 9	DATE OPENED 10	TYPE 11	TERMS 12	13	BALANCE 14	BALANCE DATE 15	AMOUNT PAST DUE 16	1 2 3 4 5 6 7 8 9 10 11 12

1 Information used to obtain this Credit Profile abbreviated in computer language
2 Your name and most recent address and reporting subscriber number, your employment on the date shown and year of birth or age, if on file
3 These columns provide an abbreviated description of the status of the items in your profile POS(Positive) Generally viewed as favorable by credit grantors NEG(Negative) Generally viewed as unfavorable by credit grantors NON(Nonevaluated) May be viewed positively, negatively or indifferently depending on each credit grantor's policy and experience A and M indicate the method by which the credit grantor reports information to TRW (M) Manual Manually prepared form (A) Automated Automated tapes prepared from the credit grantor's computer
4 Name of credit grantor, lienholder or court name
5 A TRW assigned identification number
6 An association code describes your legal relationship with an account (See below)
7 The number assigned to your account by the credit grantor or court docket number
8 Abbreviated description of the account status (See Explanation of Status Comments to the right.)
9 The status comment shown in 8 is as of this date
10 Month account opened or month credit transaction took place 5-Y or 10-Y indicates open prior to 5 years or 10 years respectively
11 Credit grantor's abbreviated description of the nature of the credit extended (See chart below)
12 Terms are the periods within which extensions of credit are to be repaid Charge accounts are stated as REV meaning revolving Terms for account types R E, R F, R V and R C (See #11) are stated in years and for all other account types the terms are stated in months
13 This amount will be either the amount of the original (or revised) credit established, or the highest amount owed
14 Balance owning on date stated under balance date (#15) or the name of judgement creditor
15 Date of the balance (#14)
16 Dollar amount past due or [illegible] lance date (#15), if any
17 This information is read fr[illegible] eft to right This column reflects the status of the account for each of the 12 months preceding the balance date (#15) A bla[illegible] ace indicates we do not maintain a payment history of this account A symbol appearing under one of the numbers (1 thr[illegible] 12) means that the account had such a status (as defined below) in that month under which the symbol appears The follow[illegible] symbols are used in this column

C	current	5	150 days past due
1	30 days past due	6	180 days past due
2	60 days past due	.	no history has been reported for that particular month
3	90 days past due		
4	120 days past due	Blank	no history maintained, see status comment

EXPLANATION OF STATUS COMMENTS

BK ADJ PLN	Debt included in or completed through Bankruptcy Chapter 13.
BK LIQ REO	Debt included in or discharged through
CHARGE OFF	Unpaid balance reported as a loss by credit grantor
CLOS INAC	Closed inactive account
CLOS NP AA	Credit line closed/not paying as agreed
COLL ACCT	Account seriously past due/account assigned to attorney, collection agency or credit grantor's internal collection department
CO NOW PAY	Now paying, was a charge-off
CR CD LOST	Credit card lost or stolen
CR LN CLOS	Credit line closed/reason unknown or by consumer request/there may be a balance due
CR LN RNST	Account now available for use and is in good standing. Was a closed account
CURR ACCT	This is either an open or closed account in good standing. If the account is a credit card or charge account, it should be available for use and there may be a balance due. If the account is closed, there were no past due amounts reported and it was paid
CUR WASCOL	Current account was a collection account
CUR WAS DL	Current account was past due
CUR WASFOR	Current account. Foreclosure was started
CUR WAS 30	Current account was 30 days past due
CURWAS30-2	Current account was 30 days past due twice
CURWAS30-3	Current account was 30 days past due three times
CURWAS30-4	Current account was 30 days past due four times
CURWAS30-5	Current account was 30 days past due five times
CURWAS30 + 6	Current account was 30 days past due six times or more
CUR WAS 60	Current account was 60 days delinquent
CUR WAS 90	Current account was 90 days delinquent
CUR WAS120	Current account was 120 days delinquent
CUR WAS150	Current account was 150 days delinquent
CUR WAS180	Current account was 180 days or more delinquent
DECEASED	Consumer deceased
DELINQ 60	Account delinquent 60 days
DELINQ 90	Account delinquent 90 days
DELINQ 120	Account delinquent 120 days
DELINQ 150	Account delinquent 150 days
DELINQ 180	Account delinquent 180 days
DEL WAS 90	Account was delinquent 90 days/now 30 or 60 days delinquent.
DEL WAS120	Account was delinquent 120 days/now 30, 60 or 90 days delinquent
EDU CLAIM	Claim filed with government for insured portion of balance on an educational loan
FORECLOSURE	Credit grantor sold collateral to settle defaulted mortgage
FORE PROC	Foreclosure proceeding started
INQUIRY	A copy of the credit profile has been sent to this credit grantor at their request
INS CLAIM	Claim filed for payment of insured portion of balance
NOT PD AA	Account not being paid as agreed
PAID ACCT	Closed account/zero balance/not rated by credit grantor
PAID SATIS	Closed account/paid satisfactory
PD BY DLER	Credit grantor paid by company who originally sold the merchandise
PD CHG OFF	Paid account/was a charge-off
PD COLL AC	Paid account/was a collection account, insurance claim or education claim
PD FORECLO	Paid account. A foreclosure was started
PD NOT AA	Paid account. Some payments were made past the agreed due dates
PD REPO	Paid account/was a repossession
PD WAS 30	Paid account/was past due 30 days
PD WAS30-2	Paid account/was past due 30 days 2 or 3 times
PD WAS30-4	Paid account/was past due 30 days 4 times
PD WAS30-5	Paid account/was past due 30 days 5 times
PD WAS30 + 6	Paid account/was past due 30 days 6 times or more
PD WAS 60	Paid account/was delinquent 60 days
PD WAS 90	Paid account/was delinquent 90 days
PD WAS 120	Paid account/was delinquent 120 days
PD WAS 150	Paid account/was delinquent 150 days
PD WAS 180	Paid account/was delinquent 180 days or more
REDMD REPO	Account was a repossession/now redeemed
REFINANCED	Account renewed or refinanced
REPO	Merchandise was taken back by credit grantor; there may be a balance due
SCNL	Credit grantor cannot locate consumer
SCNL NWLOC	Credit grantor could not locate consumer/consumer now located
SETTLED	Account legally paid in full for less than the full balance
TRANSFERRED	Account transferred to another office
VOLUN REPO	Voluntary repossession
30 DAY DEL	Account past due 30 days
30 2 TIMES	Account past due 30 days 2 times
30 3 TIMES	Account past due 30 days 3 times
30 4 TIMES	Account past due 30 days 4
30 5 TIMES	Account past due 30 days 5 times
30 6 + TIMES	Account past due 30 days 6 times or more
30 WAS 60	Account was delinquent 60 days/now 30 days

COURT CODES

CIR	CIRCUIT
CITY	CITY
CVL	CIVIL
CO	COUNTY
CT	COURT
DIS	DISTRICT
IRS	INTERNAL REVENUE SERVICE
JUS	JUSTICE
MUN	MUNICIPAL
REG	REGISTRAR
ST	STATE
SPR	SUPERIOR
SUP	SUPREME

TYPE OF ACCOUNT

ABBREV	EXPLANATION
AUT	Auto
UNS	Unsecured
SEC	Secured
P S	Partially Secured
H I	Home Improvement
FHA	FHA Home Improvement
ISC	Installment Sales Contract
CHG	Charge Account
R E	Real Estate Specific Type Unknown-term in years
SCO	Secured by Co-Signer
BUS	Business
REC	Recreational Merchandise
EDU	Educational
LEA	Lease
COM	Co-Maker (not borrower)
C C	Check Credit or Line of Credit
F C	FHA Co-Maker (not borrower)
M H	Mobile Home
CRC	Credit Card
R F	FHA Real Estate Mortgage-terms are in years
NTE	Note Loan
NCM	Note Loan with Co-Maker
HHG	Secured By Household Goods
H · C	Secured By Household Goods & Other Collateral
ASL	Auto
R V	VA Real Estate Mortgage-terms are in years
R C	Conventional Real Estate Mortgage-terms are in years
R O	Real Estate Mortgage-with or without other collateral Usually a second mortgage-terms are in months Amount shown in $100.00 increments
SLC	Co-Maker (not borrower)
REN	Rental Agreement
SUM	Summary of Accounts with same-status
UNK	Unknown
DCS	Debt Counseling Service
CCP	Combined Credit Plan
OST	Account review by credit grantor
A M	Account monitor by credit grantor
RVW	Account review by credit grantor
EMP	Employment
PSC	Solicitation

ASSOCIATION CODES WITH DEFINITIONS

ASSOCIATION WITH ACCOUNT CURRENTLY ACTIVE .... ASSOCIATION TERMINATED AS OF DATE REPORTED

0 .... UNDESIGNATED .... A

Reported by TRW Credit Data only

1 .... INDIVIDUAL ....

This individual is the only person associated with this account.

2 .... JOINT ACCOUNT-CONTRACTUAL RESPONSIBILITY .... B

This individual is expressly obligated to repay all debts arising on this account by reason of having signed an agreement to that effect. There are others associated with this account who may or may not have contractual responsibility.

3 .... AUTHORIZED USER-JOINT ACCOUNT C

This individual has use of this joint account for which another individual has contractual responsibility

4 .... JOINT ACCOUNT .... D

This individual participates in this account. The association cannot be distinguished between Joint Account-Contractual Responsibility or Authorized User.

5 .... CO-MAKER .... E

This individual has guaranteed this account and assumes responsibility should maker default. This code only to be used in conjunction with Code 7-Maker.

6 .... ON BEHALF OF .... F

This individual has signed an application for the purpose of securing credit for another individual, other than spouse.

7 .... MAKER .... G

This individual is responsible for this account, which is guaranteed by a co-maker. To be used in lieu of Code 2 and 3 when there is a Code 5-Co-Maker.

ITEMS OF PUBLIC RECORD

CH 7—FILED	Voluntary or Involuntary Petition in Bankruptcy Chapter 7 - (Liquidation) filed
CH 7—DISCH	Voluntary or Involuntary Petition in Bankruptcy Chapter 7 - (Liquidation) discharged
CH 7—DISM	Voluntary or Involuntary Petition in Bankruptcy Chapter 7 - (Liquidation) dismissed
CH 11—FILE	Voluntary or Involuntary Petition in Bankruptcy Chapter 11 - (Reorganization) filed
CH 11—DISC	Voluntary or Involuntary Petition in Bankruptcy Chapter 11 - (Reorganization) discharged
CH 11 —DISM	Voluntary or Involuntary Petition in Bankruptcy Chapter 11 - (Reorganization) dismissed
CH 13—FILE	Petition in Bankruptcy Chapt. 13 (Adjustment of Debt) filed
CH 13—DISM	Petition in Bankruptcy Chapt. 13 (Adjustment of Debt) dismissed
CH 13—COMP	Petition in Bankruptcy Chapt. 13 (Adjustment of Debt) completed
CITY TX LN	City Tax Lien
CITY TX REL	City Tax Lien Released
CONSEL SER	Debt Counseling Service
CO TAX LN	County Tax Lien
CO TAX REL	County Tax Lien Released
FED TAX LN	Federal Tax Lien
FED TX REL	Federal Tax Lien Released
JUDGMENT	Judgment
JUDGMT SAT	Judgment Satisfied
JUDG VACAT	Judgment Vacated or Reversed
MECH LIEN	Mechanic's Lien
MECH RELE	Mechanic's Lien Released
MN MTG FIL	Manual Mortgage Report (Developed credit report prepared for this credit grantor, copy attached.)
NT RESPON	Not Responsible Notice, e.g., husband or wife claims not responsible for debts incurred by spouse.
STAT TX LN	State Tax Lien
STAT TX REL	State Tax Lien Released
SUIT	Suit
SUIT DISMD	Suit Dismissed or Discontinued
WAGE ASIGN	Wage Assignment
W A RELEASE	Wage Assignment Released

or other lender who determines whether you are worthy of its credit.

- The best way to keep your credit standing is to pay your debts on time.
- Under the law, you are entitled to see any credit report on you that has been prepared by a credit bureau and to challenge any items in the report that seem incorrect. The credit bureau is obliged to make an investigation and correct any errors. This is especially important if the information or evidence could be misleading.
- Any time you are denied credit by any organization to which you have applied, you are entitled to receive a copy of your credit history free of charge. If you simply want to check into what a local credit bureau has on you in its files, the bureau may insist on a fee for issuing a copy of your report. Usually the fee is less than $10. You can find your local credit bureau by looking in the yellow pages under "Credit Reporting Agencies."

Two important credit laws

If you have any complaints about how a lender treats you, two key laws may help:

1. *The Fair Credit Billing Act.* This law sets up a procedure for correcting billing mistakes, for promptly crediting your payments, and for your refusal to make credit card payments on defective goods.

   The law defines a billing error as:
   a. any unauthorized charge from which you receive no benefit
   b. any charge for a wrong amount or a wrong date
   c. any charge that is not correctly identified
   d. any charge for which you want to see an explanation or clarification (i.e., you want to see the creditor's documentation)
   e. any charge for goods or services that were not delivered to you or were not accepted by you in accordance with your agreement with the seller (e.g., a department store delivers the right sofa in the wrong color)
   f. any failure to credit a payment to your account promptly
   g. any errors in arithmetic (e.g., the creditor incorrectly computes the finance charge)

   h. any additional finance charge or minimum payment due that results from failure by the creditor to deliver the bill to your current address (remember, however, that when you move you must notify the creditor at least 10 days before the closing date of the billing cycle involved).

What do you do if you don't agree with a bill? Procedures are outlined under the law, including:

- Notify the creditor *in writing* within 60 days after the bill was mailed. Be sure to include your name, account number, the reasons why you believe the bill contains an error, and the suspected amount of the error or the item you want explained.
- Pay all parts of the bill that you do not dispute. While you are waiting for a reply, you do not have to pay the amount in question or any minimum payments or finance charges that apply to the disputed amount.
- If it turns out that the creditor has made a mistake, you do not have to pay any finance charges on the disputed amount. Your account must be corrected, and you must be sent an explanation of any amount you still owe.
- If the creditor cannot find an error, he or she must promptly send you an explanation of the reasons for saying there is no mistake, and a statement of what you owe; this may include any finance charges that have accumulated and any minimum payments you may have missed while you were disputing the bill.

   Note: It is unlawful for a creditor to threaten your credit rating while you are resolving a billing dispute. Your creditor is not permitted to report you as delinquent, close out your account, or deduct money from other accounts to pay the disputed amount. If after the matter is settled (from the creditor's standpoint) you still disagree, write again. The creditor must report to the credit bureau that you have challenged the bill, and must give you the name and address of each person who has received information about your account. After the matter is finally settled, the creditor must report the outcome to each person who has received information about you. In addition, you are entitled to put your side of the dispute in writing in your credit history on file at the credit bureau.

The Fair Credit Billing Act also obliges your creditor to credit payments to your account on the day the payment is received at the specified address, so that you do not run up finance charges after you have sent in your payment. The creditor must also mail your bill at least 14 days before the payment is due, if your account is the type that gives you a period in which to pay before finance charges are added.

2. *The Equal Credit Opportunity Act.* Before this law was passed in 1975, there was much discrimination based on sex and marital status. It was common to deny credit to a married couple whose joint income was more than enough to carry the loan, on the grounds that the woman was of childbearing age, might become pregnant and quit work, and thus the couple's income would drop.

The act does not guarantee that you or anyone else will be issued credit. But it does prohibit discrimination based on sex, marital status, race, color, religion, national origin, age, and other factors. It requires every creditor to apply the same standards of "creditworthiness" equally to all applicants. Its most important rules:

- You cannot be denied credit because you are a woman. Before this act was passed, women had difficulty getting credit. Bankers and other creditors believed that a woman would ignore her debts when she got married, and that her income would disappear after marriage because she would leave the work force to have children.
- Single, married, separated, divorced, or widowed—none of these states can be a reason for denying you credit.
- A creditor may not refuse you credit because you depend on income from alimony or child support.

- A woman who is deemed creditworthy is not required to have her husband cosign an account (except in certain instances where property rights are involved).
- If your marital status changes, a creditor may not require you to reapply for credit, change the terms of your account, or close your account—unless there is some clear indication that you are no longer willing or able to repay your debt. In the case of a separation, divorce, or death, a creditor may ask you to reapply if your spouse's income was needed to support your credit. Thus, getting married does *not* mean that either of you must give up your own accounts or your own credit history.
- If both husband and wife use an account or are liable for it, the names of both must be carried on reports to credit bureaus (formerly, accounts were reported only in the name of the husband).
- Your creditor has just 30 days after your application has been completed in which to notify you of approval or denial. If you are denied credit, the notice must be in writing and must tell you why.
- If your account is closed, you have the same rights: You must be notified in writing, with the reason clearly stated.

   Note: If you are denied credit, be sure to find out—and *understand*—why. Some possible reasons: You may have asked for more money than the creditor feels you can repay on your income and considering your other obligations...you may not have lived in the community long enough, or been on your job long enough...you don't have a credit record or history.

   Important: If you have reason to believe you have been discriminated against, cite the law. And dig in and fight.

How much credit is too much?

Your budget answers this question. It will tell you how much credit you can safely afford to carry. To start using credit without setting up a working budget is foolhardy. If you aren't watching where your money is going, you can get into trouble before you

Worksheet VII: The Nicholses
LIST OF DEBTS

Date _____

CREDITOR'S NAME	TYPE OF LOAN	DATE OF LAST PAYMENT	MATURITY DATE	MONTHLY PAYMENT From Budget	TOTAL AMOUNT DUE From Net Worth Statement
ABC Credit	auto	current	3/15/93	257	4,000
Autoland USA	auto	current	10/1/94	206	5,000
MasterCard	revolving acc't			current	
VISA	revolving acc't			current	
Student Loan ~ Eric			12/95	50	2,500
Student Loan ~ Jeanne			12/95	50	2,500

TOTAL MONTHLY PAYMENTS $563

TOTAL AMOUNT OWED _____ $14,000

know it. Most credit counselors agree that most people could avoid excessive debt by simply budgeting their money.

"Over–extended" is the term the banker types like to use. The scenario goes like this: Your checking account balance drops to zero. Your wallet or purse is empty. You want to—or need to—buy something. Out comes the credit card and up goes your credit–card balance. Each month your payment gets larger. Your balance tops out at the limit originally approved by your bank. You apply for more credit. Or you go to other stores and open new accounts.

Eventually in this scenario, your minimum payments plus the finance charges on a number of accounts get to be one of your major monthly items of expense, cutting ever more deeply into each month's available cash for discretionary and other uses. You miss a monthly payment or two, because now you're juggling—paying this account this month, that account next month. Past due notices are arriving regularly in the mail. Next: phone calls and notices from collection agencies.

You don't have to be a $100,000–a–year executive to find yourself playing this ulcer–producing scene. Plenty of $18,000–a–year secretaries and assistant managers have debts as high as their annual pay. It's no fun.

And here are some of the possible consequences. Your creditor can:

- repossess the merchandise—come and haul away the furniture or drive away the car; they are not yours until *all* payments have been made
- take away the collateral you put up to secure the loan
- garnishee your wages—get a legal lien that forces your employer to give your creditor up to 10 percent of your pay each pay period until the debt is repaid.
- tell the credit bureaus—providing negative information about you that the credit bureau will show to other creditors.

How do you determine how much credit you can handle? You must find out what your *debt ratio* is, and see whether it is comfortably low, safely just about right, or uncomfortably high—and, if it's too high, work to get it down.

Turn to Worksheet VII, marked **List of Debts**, and to Worksheet VIII, **Personal Debt Ratio**. Fill in all debts that are current (your total indebtedness is on your Net Worth Statement; your monthly obligations are included under credit repayment on your fixed–expense sheet).

Use the Debt Ratio sheet to figure out a ratio for yourselves, based on total take–home pay and installment obligations. Your debt ratio is a percentage of your total take–home pay (the net income you have on your budget sheet, after all payroll deductions) that is committed to repaying your debts.

Most people are in danger if they commit more than 15 to 20 percent of net income to paying debt. If the ratio goes higher, you may find yourselves sliding into the scenario of robbing Peter to pay Paul and charging items that have a life span less than the time it takes to pay for them.

Here's a good standard to apply: Can all your debts be paid off in 18 to 24 months? If not, your debt ratio is too high.

At any particular time, you should know the ratio of all your debts to your total net income. It will change, of course, when you pay off a loan—and you can then decide whether it is safe to borrow again, and how much it makes sense to borrow.

Turn to the completed Worksheets VII and VIII Jeanne and Eric Nichols filled out. Figuring out their debt ratio, they realize they are devoting 15.2 percent of their net income to repaying debt. With two car loans and student loans, they know they can't afford to take on any more consumer debt while they are saving for the house they want so very much.

Tip: Resist the inclination, when you have just paid off a loan that had an obligation of $50 a month, to take on another with a $65 monthly payment. You say to yourselves, "What's another $15 a month—we can handle that." But if you have other expenses that are rising, and if inflation is creeping up, what looks like "a mere $15" can be disastrous. Adding a new debt that is higher than the old one each time is a sure way to get into a dangerous debt ratio. Keeping debt within your means, on the other hand, will give you more spendable dollars as you avoid paying out a large amount for interest.

The spending habit: Can you kick it?

It's tough, but you can do it. Your best way is to go cold turkey. If your budget, your cash flow analysis, and your debt ratio all show that you have just plain got to cut back on expenses in order to pay off debt, make an agreement with each other that you will not—absolutely and positively will not—add any new debts for at least one year.

You might even take your charge cards and put them in a friend's safe–deposit box. Or cut them in half and return them to the creditor, with a note of explanation.

Then cast a cold eye on your budget. Cut out—or at least cut down on—every living expense that is not an absolute necessity. Open another savings account and put a certain amount in every day, using this account for debt reduction and *only* for debt reduction.

Sounds impossible? I've seen it work time and again. With this kind of regimen, you can learn—together—to manage on the amount of money you have.

If you are having trouble paying your loans, let your creditors be the first to know. A job loss, illness or a death in the family are understood by creditors. They might rewrite the loans, extending your time and thus reducing the monthly payments. A creditor would rather extend your loan than receive nothing at all.

If you can't kick the habit on your own, there are nonprofit consumer–credit counseling agencies across the country. These services are supported by state and local governments, businesses and creditors. Some of the services charge a small one–time fee while others have a small monthly fee. A credit counselor will have you keep a record of every penny that you are spending to discover where your leaks are. You are then given a pair of scissors to cut up your credit cards. A repayment schedule is worked out, based on what you can afford to pay back and not what you promised to pay back. You then make one monthly payment to the agency, which in turn makes payments to the creditors on your behalf.

If you're in deep trouble, you can find lending institutions that will consolidate all your debts, lending you enough to pay back everyone you owe. You then pay back that lender over an extended period. The trouble is, it's expensive, as this type of loan may involve a substantial amount of interest. But it gives you a lower amount to pay each month—lower than the total of paying all those separate accounts—for debt reduction.

If you're into that kind of debt reduction plan—consolidating all your debts—don't make the mistake of starting to use your plastic cards all over again before the big consolidated loan is paid off. If you do, you'll start the cycle again and, within a few months or a year or two, you'll be signing for another consolidation loan. This is the path to bankruptcy.

What about bankruptcy?

I don't want you even to think about it. But this book would be incomplete if it did not explain the basics. Some facts, tips and suggestions:

- Congress passed the Bankruptcy Reform Act of 1978 to ease the burdens of going bankrupt and to make it easier to repay a substantial portion of one's debt. The law recognizes the fact that people often get themselves into economic situations that are beyond their control. The "ripple effect" of inflation, for example, is tough on those who are overextended. The Bankruptcy Act has resulted in a tremendous increase in the numbers of personal bankruptcies, with creditors losing about $6 billion.
- Talk with a lawyer before you decide to declare personal bankruptcy. Get yourselves informed on various "chapters" of the Bankruptcy Act. Some details you'll learn:
  - You must get petitions filled out.
  - Chapter 7 covers a "straight bankruptcy" in which the court collects, sells and distributes debtors' assets.
  - Chapter 13 encourages debtors to repay their loans.
  - Chapter 13, the so–called "wage–earner plan," allows you to consolidate debts and repay a court–approved percentage of them over three years.
  - Creditors must suspend charges for interest or late payments on most debts.
  - Creditors are barred from continuing any action against the debtors.
  - If you use Chapter 13 and then default on payments, the court will throw you into Chapter 7 proceedings.

How to stay out of credit trouble

Keep these points in mind:

1. Debt must be paid off; paying a loan is a fixed expense.

2. Deferred spending is often avoided spending. Ask yourselves: Would we buy this if we had the cash in hand to buy it?
3. Good axiom about small purchases: If you can't afford to pay cash, you can't afford to buy it on credit.
4. Always shop around before signing for a loan.
5. Avoid impulse shopping. If you have to buy something to "lift your spirits," keep within reason.
6. Never put everyday expenses on credit.
7. Watch credit card purchases closely. Make sure you both put credit card slips in one place immediately after any purchase. There's nothing worse than opening a monthly credit card bill to learn for the first time that your spouse has added a large purchase.

Almost "free" money

Your credit cards can be the closest thing you will ever have to "free" money. Here's how:

The best way to use credit cards is to pay the full amount due every month. Usually your credit card allows a grace period of 25 to 30 days from the date when you are billed until you will be assessed interest or a finance charge. So if you make a purchase immediately after your billing date (which is imprinted on your bill), and if you pay in full when you pay, you can gain free credit for almost two months. *Example:* Suppose your billing date is July 1. If you buy something on July 2, it will not appear on your bill until August, and you will then have until September 1 (or the stated due date) to pay for that purchase. If you pay the full amount of your new balance by September, no interest will be charged. You will have had free use of your July 2 purchase until the first of September.

Understanding finance charges

Finance charges are added to any credit card bill if the amount due is not paid in full. The charges can be calculated by any number of methods.

The most common method is the *average daily balance method with newly billed purchases included.* This method does not allow the grace period for newly purchased items that I talked about in describing "almost 'free' money." Under this method, it is important to note that the finance charge is based on the average amount you have charged during the month. As soon as your latest purchase goes into the computer, your average changes and your finance charge increases. The finance charge then continues to be calculated on your latest average daily balance until it again changes. Therefore, if your creditor is using this method, it is better to pay as soon as you receive the bill, rather than waiting (as you might have done when paying in full) until the end of the month. In other words, if you decide to leave part of a bill unpaid for just one month, you will be charged interest.

The cost of stretching out payments

If you make only partial payments month after month, you are using a very costly method of repaying your debts. Here's why.

Whatever amount you pay, the creditor takes the full finance charge out before crediting anything to your account. This means that if you pay only the minimum due, you reduce the actual amount you owe by that amount *less* the finance charge. Say you send in the minimum payment of $50 called for on your monthly statement. If the finance charge on the *total* that you owe is $10, the creditor will take $10 to pay that finance charge and thus deduct only $40 from the total you owe. So if the balance you owe is quite large, your required minimum payment may be mostly interest (i.e, finance charge) month after month. The principal amount you owe will be reduced ever so slowly—much too slowly for you to consider it sound money management.

> *Tip:* One practical way to use multipurpose cards (VISA, MasterCard) is to put all big–ticket items on one, and all small–cost items on the other. Then be sure to pay the card with the small–cost items in full every month. That gives you the convenience of buying the shirt or the lipstick with plastic—while you're paying for the stereo over the long haul. *Caution:* This system works only if you pay up—promptly and in full—on the small–cost account every month.

Student loans—and Sallie Mae Options

Is either of you—or are you both—repaying a student loan? Are the repayments using up most of your debt ratio? If so, you must put the brakes on other debt obligations *and* get a good understanding of student loans.

First some background. If you borrowed for college or graduate school under the Guaranteed Student Loan Program (GSL), National Direct Student Loans (NDSL), or Federally Insured Student Loans (FISL), you were allowed very low interest rates through a bank or credit union. The loans were insured either by the federal government or the guarantee agency in your state. Your rate of interest was set with the first loan you received, and all your subsequent loans stayed at that rate even if interest rates rose. Your maximum repayment period was to be either 10 years or 15 years from the date of your first loan. If student loans are, in fact, a heavy part of your debt ratio, that's a long haul.

Now, meet Sallie Mae. That's a nickname for the Student Loan Marketing Association (SLMA, or Sallie Mae). In 1981, Sallie Mae set up a program called OPTIONS to help former students stretch out their repayment of student loans. The Sallie Mae OPTIONS program:

- consolidates all your loans (perhaps one a year for several college years) into a single debt
- gives you a lower monthly payment
- gives you a choice: equal payments over the years, or graduated payments that increase as your earning power increases
- gives you up to 20 years to repay
- lets you wait until six months after you leave college before you must start payments
- restricts eligibility to loans that are not delinquent or in default, but lets you become eligible by bringing payments up to date
- lets you apply for options at any time
- may be used on any loan or combination of loans that is more than $7,500
- may be used if your loans total more than $5,000 from more than one lender (i.e., you attended two or more different schools).

Suppose you owe a total of $12,000 in student loans. Under the regular payment plan, the term is 10 years and your monthly payment of interest and principal is $140. Under the Sallie Mae OPTIONS program, you have these choices.

Option 1. Equal payments during the repayment term. Your debt would be extended to 16 years, with monthly payments reduced to about $104. Good for keeping the budget under control.

Option 2. Graduated payments, starting at a low level and increasing. Maximum period would also be 16 years, but payments would increase every two years from $79 a month at the start to about $152 in the final years. Helpful if you're just starting on your career.

Option 3. Payments accelerating more rapidly than in Option 2. Maximum period would be 13.3 years, with payments increasing every two years— from $79 at the start to about $189 at the end. Great if you expect your income to rise fast.

For each option, the interest rate is fixed at seven percent annually. If your interest rate is now less than seven percent—for instance, on a National Direct Student Loan—the Sallie Mae OPTIONS program could cost you more while giving you a longer time to pay. If you have a nine percent Guaranteed Student loan, you would save on interest.

Sallie May can be a big help. The reduction in monthly expenses it can provide may make it possible for you to borrow to buy a car, for instance, or simply add to the flexibility of your budget.

So weigh the options. Decide whether it is better to extend the time of repayment, despite greater interest charges, in order to keep the size of monthly payments within your budget.

Then, if you want to apply for a Sallie Mae OPTION, write to:

Sallie Mae
Student Loan Consolidation Center
P.O. Box 973
Beltsville, MD 20705

Include information on who your lenders were, which programs you are in (GSL, NDSL, or FISL), the amount you now owe on each, the date repayment on each began or will begin, the total number of loans you have signed for (and total number of lenders), and the total amount you owe.

You can get a lot of benefits from credit. It lets you go places and buy things you might otherwise never be able to see or own, or that it would take you years to save for. But you must handle credit carefully. Budgeting is your most valuable tool for knowing how much credit you can comfortably afford to carry, and it is the only way to control credit abuse and—if abuse occurs—take charge and get it back under control.

It boils down to this: You control credit or credit controls you. Take your choice.

Worksheet VII: Yours
LIST OF DEBTS

Date _____

CREDITOR'S NAME	TYPE OF LOAN	DATE OF LAST PAYMENT	MATURITY DATE	MONTHLY PAYMENT From Budget	TOTAL AMOUNT DUE From Net Worth Statement

TOTAL MONTHLY PAYMENTS $

TOTAL AMOUNT OWED $

Worksheet VIII: Yours
PERSONAL DEBT RATIO

Your ratio is based on take-home pay. You have figured out the amount of debt that you owe for installment loans. Is this too much for you?

		Monthly	**Yearly**
1.	Your total take-home pay	$	
2.	Use 15% (a safe amount for most consumers). Divide income by 6.7 or use 20% (maximum for most consumers). Divide by 5.	$	
3.	Your present installment obligations	$	
4.	Your present safety margin—subtract line 3 from line 2.	$	
5.	Your present ratio—divide your installments obligation (line 3) by your take-home pay (line 1).	$	

It might be wise to use both the 15% and 20% figures to see the difference in your own situation.

YOUR JOB AND YOUR FRINGE BENEFITS

9

Almost any older couple you ask will tell you that job changes are a part of life when you are young and especially, it seems, when you are newly married. It's a time when you are looking for opportunities to connect—to land the ideal spot in the ideal company in the field you have chosen, or maybe even to move into a related field.

When you are considering a job change or actually starting a new job, fringe benefits can make a big difference. These are all the "extras" that most employers offer in addition to your regular pay, and include life insurance and medical insurance, dental plans, and retirement plans. You need to check them carefully, for you can get burned just as easily as you can come out far better than on your last job. A beautiful pay increase, for instance, could be offset by a real loss in fringe benefits. Moving from a company that pays all Blue Cross premiums in full to one that deducts them from your paycheck could be a mistake if you don't pick up enough of a pay increase to cover the difference. In fact, a top–notch fringe benefit package can be worth the equivalent of hundreds of thousands of dollars more in compensa-

tion, over the long haul. Some companies that pay low salaries are extremely generous with fringe benefits. They find it's one good way to keep turnover down. If both spouses work, you should check your respective coverages. The chances are you will find duplication in your employee benefit programs. Look over your benefits and your spouse's very carefully to be sure you don't pay for double coverage.

Let's take a look at some of the items that are included in a fringe–benefit package.

Insurance

Most companies carry several types of insurance for their employees, deducting the family premiums (or a percentage of them) from the regular paycheck. By putting all its employees together in a single group, the company gets a rate, or price, that is much lower than any individual could get. Typical coverage includes:

- *Life insurance.* Most employers provide life insurance. Usually your coverage is one to two times your annual pay. In some companies, you can buy additional coverage at the low group rate, with the premium deducted from your paycheck. This could be extremely valuable if, for example, you have a medical problem that makes you uninsurable or necessitates extra premium riders on life insurance polices, for, if you are in a company group, you do not have to pass an individual physical examination to determine your eligibility. Find out the cost of optional insurance within your company's plan. Then check with outside agents. You may find it cheaper to buy from an outside agent, especially if you are under 30. Very often a younger worker is subsidizing the insurance costs of older employees.

> *Important:* When you leave your company for another job, you leave your group life insurance behind. Usually, however, you are entitled to convert your group policy within a month to an individual policy for which you pay the insurance company directly—again, without a physical exam but at a higher premium.

- *Health and dental insurance.* Probably there are more variations among company attitudes on these fringes than on life insurance. Some companies, for instance, pay Blue Cross in full for their employees, while others pass the full cost along through payroll deductions (you get an advantage, nevertheless, because you are paying your share of a group premium rather than an individual policy premium). Some companies pay for the employee's coverage but not for his or her dependents. Others pay for Blue Cross but not for major-medical coverage.

If each of you has health coverage on the job, you need to investigate the provisions of each. If the coverage is free or has a minimal charge, you will probably not want to drop either one. You could then coordinate your benefits. By submitting your claims to both insurance companies, for instance, you can recover up to 100 percent of your medical expenses.

Here's how it works: You each enroll in your own plan as an employee, and then you name your spouse as a dependent. If the cost is high, you might carry only the policy that provides the best coverage for the lowest price. To determine that, compare deductibles and the percentage of the medical bills you have to pay under each plan. Be sure to enroll your children in the plan that gives you the best coverage. Important: Don't drop either coverage until you have worked it all out. Some questions to ask:

How much, if anything, do employees themselves have to pay?

Must the employee pay for dependents?

What is the deductible allowed for the employee and family?

Is there a maximum yearly limit on the dollar amount of claims—or on their number?

Are there any medical problems that this kind of insurance does not cover?

Just what does the dental plan cover? (Some may not include routine cleaning by a dental hygienist; most pay less than the standard fees charged by most practicing dentists for bridges and for orthodontic work—i.e., braces.)

- *Disability insurance.* Most people give very little thought to short–term disability coverage, yet you need only one accident to understand its importance. The chances of becoming disabled for several weeks or for three months or more are high. If your company does not offer disability coverage, you can buy a policy on your own.

> *Note:* All of the foregoing on insurance is discussed here simply to give you the basics of insurance *as a fringe benefit*. (See Chapter 11 for details on types of insurance, how much you should buy, how long–term and short–term disability plans work, and many other practical tips.)

Savings plans

The payroll system where you work can help you to save. Many companies offer a straight payroll savings plan. This sets aside a certain amount to be deducted from every paycheck, or once a month, and put directly into a savings account.

One plan gives you a way to save money and actually get more take–home pay at the same time. Called a *salary reduction plan*, it permits you to deduct part of your salary every year, up to a maximum of $7,627, *before* the company pays any withholding taxes on it. Thus the money saved is pre–tax, rather than after–tax, dollars. The money put into this type of account, called a 401(k), is deferred on a tax–sheltered basis so it can accumulate until you leave the company or retire.

Here's how it works: Say you are earning $25,000 a year. You could choose a 6 percent salary reduction. The company sets aside $1,500 ($25,000 × 6 percent) over a year and figures your withholding taxes on the basis of a salary of $23,500. The salary reduction plan:

- reduces state and city income taxes
- can grow rapidly if your employer kicks in (as many do) 50 percent of the amount you are contributing
- is not sealed in concrete; if you get into a jam and need the money that's been put away, you can take advantage of the plan's hardship provision
- if you decide that only one of you will join a 401(k) plan, go with the one that gives higher matching by the employer.

Retirement benefits

You may think the last thing you want to be concerned about now is retirement plans. But this is one very important benefit. You should understand it. Find out, first of all, whether you are covered by your company's retirement plan. Some companies limit their plans to those who have certain jobs and work a certain specified number of hours, or those who have been with the company for a certain period of time or have reached a certain age. You can also be included in a plan but not yet eligible to receive any benefits from it. For example, take "vesting." When you are vested in a pension plan, it means that the money credited to your name is legally yours, without question or qualification. You will get it when you retire, and if you should leave your job before then you will be entitled to take it all or, in some cases, a percentage depending on how many years you have been vested.

In most companies, you become *fully* vested only after you have worked a certain number of years (e.g., five years); or you start to be *partially* vested at various percentages over a number of years, starting sooner (e.g., after three years). Suppose you are vested after the fifth year, and the company has been putting money in since the end of your second year. And suppose a job offer from another company turns up just at the end of your fourth year. You might figure out that it would be better to wait a couple of years before changing jobs, in order to be able to take with you the money that will then be vested for you. It is important to remember that payment of vested benefits to a participant before he or she reaches the plan's retirement age is not required. Thus, if you leave employment before retirement, you may not be entitled to receive your vested benefit right away.

Some employers have "non–contributory" plans, meaning that you do not have to contribute anything; the company puts in all the money. Others use "contributory" plans, in which you must make contributions through payroll deductions. The number and types of plans are bewildering, but all fall into two basic types:

1. *Defined benefit plan.* This type specifies in advance the benefits you will receive. They may be based on the amount of your earnings over a specified period of service with the company. Or they may be a fixed dollar amount paid for each year of service.
2. *Defined contribution plan.* Here, a predetermined formula may set a fixed dollar amount as the contribution each year. Or the employer's contribution may vary from year to year as profits of the firm vary.

"Cafeteria" benefits

Here's a new breed of cat. Some companies are beginning to let employees pick and choose certain benefits—the idea growing out of the increasing number of both–spouses–working families, where certain benefits (such as Blue Cross) are often duplicated by the employers of each. Under the "cafeteria" plan, if your wife or husband is covered for a medical plan, you might decide to drop your own medical but pick up a dental plan, an extra week's vacation, additional life insurance, or maybe even cash. An employee who is young might pass up contributions to a pension plan, under the cafeteria system, and add vacation time, while an older employee might want to increase medical coverage and payments into the pension plan. You can see the possibilities—especially if you don't need many of the benefits offered where you work, because your spouse gets them for both of you at his or her place, and if you're given the option of taking cash. Not bad.

Tips:
- Always evaluate fringe benefits carefully before you start a job or change jobs.
- Investigate the "benefit" dollars as well as the "paycheck" dollars you're being offered.
- Remember that a large pay increase may well be offset by a loss of important fringe benefits.
- Fringe benefits do not usually increase your tax bill the way a salary increase will.

Check to see if your company has a "reimbursement account." Money is withheld from your paycheck on a pre–tax basis, and you use that money to pay such unreimbursed expenses as health, child–care and educational expenses—expenses you would normally pay with after–tax dollars. Think of a reimbursement account as your own personal bank account that you use periodically to reimburse yourself for specific expenses.

Here's how a Health–Care Reimbursement Account works. You specify the amount you wish to set aside for the coming year, and that amount is deducted in equal installments from your paycheck—before taxes—for deposit into your reimbursement account. How do you decide how much to put in? Consider the health–related expenses you routinely incur that are not covered by medical and dental insurance. Review last year's expenses. Consider including medical and dental deductibles, medical and dental co–payments, health–care premiums, and such uncovered medical expenses as routine physicals, vision and hearing and preventive care. The total unreimbursed expenses, or a portion of them, if you prefer, are what you will contribute to your Health–Care Reimbursement Account. Important: Federal law requires that any money left in this special account at the end of the year stays with the company. So you have to figure out in advance what your out–of–pocket costs for these benefits might be. By using this payroll deduction method, you make sure that those expenses are paid.

A Dependent Day–Care Reimbursement Account allows you to be reimbursed for expenses incurred, while you are gainfully employed, for a dependent child under age 15 who qualifies as your tax dependent or for anyone you claim as a tax dependent because of a physical or mental inability to care for himself or herself. You decide how much to put into this account when you enroll. Under present tax law, the amount by which you may reduce your salary is limited to $5,000. The amount you designate is deducted from your paycheck in regular installments and deposited into your account. Again, remember that Federal law requires that you forfeit all unused funds, so plan your contributions carefully.

To withdraw money from the account, you complete a reimbursement request and present appropriate bills or receipts. Reimbursement checks will be mailed directly to you, not to the provider. Should you submit a request that exceeds the balance in your account, all the money in your account will be paid to you. As more funds are deposited into your account, they will automatically be paid to you until the amount of your request has been fully paid or you stop contributing.

Two very important things to remember:

1. Health–care expenses cannot be reimbursed from a Dependent–Care Account, nor vice versa.
2. If you don't use up all account balances by the end of the year, you forfeit them.

THE BUCKS ARE BOTH COVERED BY BENEFITS

The Bucks have good fringe benefits—but with a lot of duplication. Both their employers provide major medical insurance and life insurance. Pat has a good dental plan that covers Karen and the children as well. He also has disability insurance—which Karen doesn't.

Pat is contributing 10 percent of his income to a 410(k) plan, and the company contributes as well. This has built up a good nest egg. The company is thinking of starting a reimbursement account that Pat could use for child care. If it does, he could reduce his taxable income by $5,000.

A ROOF OVER YOUR HEAD

10

Owning a home is as American as Mom, apple pie, and the stars and stripes. To own your own home is the culmination of the American dream. It is a symbol of financial security, of having made it. It is also probably the best single investment available to the average American, because the house bought for $20,000 some 25 years ago is now worth (if it has been maintained well) $100,000 or more, depending on location. The only problem is that, for you and many other couples, inflation and high interest rates have made homeownership nearly impossible. Homeownership has declined over the last 10 years for people between the ages of 25 and 29. The decline is due to the high cost of purchasing that first home, which has a median price today of $115,000.

What are the advantages of homeownership? These three are basic:

1. It is your best chance to accumulate tangible capital. It is an investment you can walk around, improve, add to.

2. It is one of the few almost foolproof ways to shield an investment from inflation. (Real estate values are a barometer of economic changes.)

3. It gives you tax advantages. By allowing you to lower your income taxes through itemized deductions of the interest you pay on your mortgage and the taxes you pay on the property, your Uncle Sam provides an indirect subsidy for your house.

Today you must ask yourselves a lot of questions and do a lot of figuring before you can determine how much house you can afford. Start with this checklist, and make notes as you go, for you are sure to come up with more questions than these— questions that pertain to your own particular situation.

1. How large a down payment can we make? Obviously, the more you can put down, the lower your monthly payments will be.

2. How long a mortgage term should we sign for? Mortgages can be set up to span 20, 25, or 30 years; the shorter the period, the less you spend on interest but the higher your payments will be.

3. How large a monthly payment can we comfortably make? Your budget determines this. After you have figured out how much you need for non–housing expenses (including savings and an emergency fund), what is left is what you have to work with for housing. But remember: Insurance, utilities, property taxes, and maintenance are part of your monthly housing costs, too. This question also calls for plenty of thoughtful long–term planning. Look not only at what you are both making now but how much more you can reasonably expect if you get raises regularly…at what will happen to your joint income when you have a baby and one spouse leaves the work force either temporarily or permanently…at what the cost of child care, if necessary, will do to your budget.

4. What does the location of the home we are buying do to our expenses? Will we be adding commuting costs? A major increase in the weekly mileage on one—or two—cars? Where are the stores? Services? Recreational facilities? Will we have to drive five miles to get a loaf of bread?

5. Just how much will utilities add to the monthly housing expense? What about heat? Heat was part of the deal in a rented apartment. Now you'll have to pay for it. Better check with the fuel company that has been supplying the house and see how much fuel was used last winter—or the last two or three winters, so you can average it out.

6. How much more will insurance cost? It is bound to be greater than what you have been paying to cover your apartment.

7. How much will the property taxes be? This one can be ticklish. Find out when the last reassessment occurred. If it's been a while, another could come around soon and hit you with an unexpected hike in taxes after you move in. Check with a resident who is knowledgeable about what the local policy is. Or call the town or city hall.

8. What local services do we get? Are they free? Do our local taxes pay for garbage collection, or will we get a monthly bill from the garbage collector?

9. Are there child–care facilities nearby?

10. How are the schools? This could be the most important question on your list. If you are planning to raise a family in this house, take the time and trouble to investigate the schools thoroughly. Stop in at the school superintendent's office, or at any school principal's office, and ask questions. What is the average ratio of pupils to teacher in the classroom? How much does the community spend each year per pupil—and where does it rank among cities and towns in your state? What percentage of the high school graduates move on to higher education? Some basic demographic statistics about the school system can tell you a lot about whether or not you really should be buying this home.

11. What about the closing costs? At the time of the closing you may have to pay some "points." This is a one–time expense. Each point equals one percent of your mortgage ($1,000 on a $100,000 mortgage). Most lenders charge two to three points. A mortgage with a higher interest rate might have less points than a mortgage with a lower interest rate. And don't forget about title and mortgage insurance, attorney's fees, title search, prepayment of taxes and insurance, credit report and appraisal. You should figure closing costs of 2.5 to 3.5 percent of the amount of the mortgage.

12. Do we have sufficient reserves to pay the cost of moving and to buy those incidentals that we may not realize we need until we actually start to live in the house: fuel, insulation, lawn mower, garden hose, gardening tools, rake, snow shovel? How about landscaping? If you are buying a brand–new house, it is likely to come with a minimum of trees and shrubs. And a new house will probably lack screens, storm windows, and storm doors.

A lot to think about? You bet. But the amazing thing is—millions of Americans have survived the entire process.

How much for a down payment?

If you have asked yourselves all these questions and have come up with a firm "yes" on the ultimate one: "Can we afford a house?" you must now produce the down payment.

Let's say you have worked hard to put away $200 every month for five years. Assuming 10 percent interest on your money, compounded quarterly, you should have $15,084.83 salted away. This should give you enough for a down payment of $10,000, with the balance to be used for closing costs, moving, and all the incidentals I've mentioned. You have watched the pot grow—and now you can put it to work! The next question is: What type of housing? House and lot? Condominium? Cooperative Apartment? Mobile home? Let's look at each.

House and lot

Any house you look at is going to be either new—or old. If you're looking at a new house, you are pretty much assured that everything will function properly. The builder should stand behind the work. Furnace and appliances will come with guarantees. You may have plenty to do in the area of landscaping and perhaps painting the interior, if it has been left undecorated.

If it is an older house, you will want to be sure it is in acceptable condition. It takes expertise to evaluate an older home; don't hesitate to get it. If you are not an expert yourself, pay a professional to make an inspection. Don't just ask a friend. This will give you a reliable check on plumbing, heating, paint condition, roof, electrical wiring, insulation—a million and one details that could make the difference between frustration and satisfaction for you as buyers. Nothing is worse than having to buy a new roof or a new septic field for a house just after you bought the house itself. If the inspection reveals that something is wrong you can start to renegotiate the price with the seller, taking into account the cost you face in fixing the problem.

Condominium

The condo is rather new on the American homeowning scene. It is usually a structure on the order of an apartment house, in which you are deeded the title to,
or ownership of, your unit. It becomes your property. You also own a proportionate interest in the common facilities, such as hallways, grounds, elevators, and recreational areas (tennis courts, swimming pool, even a golf course in some condos). Each month, you pay common charges that cover taxes on the property (the tax portion of your common charge is deductible on your income tax return), maintenance, heat, and utilities. Warning: Common charges have a way of increasing, so make sure your budget is elastic enough to accept increases in them. As owners, you will join a condominium association in which each member has one vote when decisions about the condominium must be made (all members will have agreed to abide by the provisions of a condo agreement).

As a condo owner, you have the same advantages as the owner of a house and lot. Your equity builds up as time goes by (generally, condos have appreciated to match inflation, just like houses). The tax benefits that you can itemize on your income tax return are the same. Your responsibility for repairs and maintenance within your individual unit is also the same as in a house. And, generally speaking, you are entitled to sell your unit to anyone you choose.

Tips: Watch the recreational facilities. Don't be fooled into buying into a condo where the swimming pool and tennis courts are "going to be built soon." And turn your back on any place that has a tiny swimming pool or a single tennis court for a hundred condo units.

Cooperatives

In a co–op apartment, a non–profit corporation owns your unit. What you own is stock in the corporation. The amount of stock you own depends on the size and value of the apartment you take. There is one common mortgage on the building (unless the corporation has bought the building outright or already paid off the mortgage) and all the owners make monthly payments, varying in size according to the value of the individual units, to the corporation. These payments cover, in effect, taxes, interest payment, and maintenance. As a shareholder, you are entitled to list as deductions on your income tax return your share of the property taxes and the interest on the mortgage. When you want to "sell the apartment," you are really selling your shares in the corporation. *Note:* Some co–ops stipulate that any prospective owner must be approved by the other shareholders. The corporation may exercise the option of buying back the shares if the prospective owner isn't approved.

Some questions to ask before you buy into a co–op or purchase a condo:

- What are the rules and regulations? Do you want to agree to abide by them?
- Are those now living there pleased with the living conditions? Is the place noisy? Too hot? Too cold?
- Is it clean and well maintained, indoors and out? Trees and shrubs healthy? Lawn green and manicured?
- Are the recreational facilities adequate? Well maintained?
- How's the parking? Plenty of room?
- What about lighting? Parking areas well lighted? Paths and entryways clear and bright?
- Who pays for utilities? How are the costs apportioned?
- Are you permitted to rent your unit?
- What are the costs of settlement?
- Are there any lawsuits pending against the developer or officers of the association?
- Are most owners living on the premises—or have they rented out their units?

Mobile homes

This is probably the cheapest form of homeownership. It can be your first way—maybe for now your only way—to own low–cost housing.

Here's how it works. Either (1) you rent a small piece of property in an "open" park, then have your manufactured house installed on that property at your own expense, or (2) you buy a home from the management of a "closed" park. This is what many retired people do. In fact, many closed mobile–home parks are designed mainly for retired people.

In some parks, the mobile–home owners may buy their land instead of renting it. This has a certain advantage: If your mobile home is set up on your own land, some banks will offer you a regular real estate mortgage. Otherwise, they want you to finance the purchase of your mobile home like an auto loan, with a low down payment, short repayment period of three to five years at best, and high monthly pay-

ments. Recently, the U.S. government has begun insuring mobile–home loans through the Federal Housing Administration (FHA) and the Veterans Administration (VA).

A mobile home may well be a viable start for you. Before buying one, check with a number of lenders about the type of financing they offer. It's worth the effort to find the best possible deal.

Financing

You've analyzed the possibilities. You've got the down payment. You've reviewed your budget and tried to answer the nagging questions about the future. You've decided to do it. Now, how do you finance the purchase of the home you want?

Very few can come up with the full purchase price of a home. So they buy with the help of some kind of mortgage financing. Banks now look at debt–to–income ratios. Mortgage debt, which includes property taxes and homeowners insurance, should not exceed more than 28 percent of total household income. The bank will also look at total debt—mortgage debt plus such other monthly debt obligations as car payments and student loans. This ratio should not exceed 36 percent. These ratios usually apply to buyers who have 10 percent of the purchase price for the down payment. Some lenders will let you have financing with a down payment of as little as 5 percent. This means that if you have very little debt and a spotless credit history, you can buy a house sooner. Usually, because they figure you have a higher risk of defaulting on your mortgage, such lenders will say that your mortgage debt must not go over 25 percent, and your total debt not over 33 percent—rather than the 28 and 36 percent limitations mentioned above.

Just what is a "mortgage?" By definition, it is simply a pledge of property to a creditor as security for a loan. As the borrower, you are the mortgagor. You give the mortgage to the lender, or mortgagee, who takes the mortgage and holds it until you have paid the debt.

A mortgage has three elements: the amount the lender provides, the repayment period, and the rate of interest. Until very recently, once a mortgage loan was closed, none of these elements could be changed. You "got a mortgage" for a certain number of years at a certain rate of interest and that was it—period. But lately lenders, finding themselves stuck for years with mortgages that bring them low payments of interest at a time when they have to pay out high interest on savings deposited with them, have been eager to adapt to changing conditions. The result is that today you may choose between the old–fashioned conventional fixed–rate mortgage and a new type, the adjustable–rate mortgage (ARM). Let's look at each.

1. *The conventional fixed–rate mortgage.* With this type you pay a fixed monthly payment, at a fixed rate of interest, for the life of the loan—as long as 25 to 30 years. Many banks still offer the fixed–rate mortgage, but today the cost is likely to be initially higher—maybe 2.5 percent higher—than the cost of an adjustable–rate mortgage. If interest rates do go up over the long haul, you get the advantage and the bank, or lender, finds that it has loaned you money at a lower rate of return, or profit, than it might have gained by some other investment.

2. *The variable– or adjustable–rate mortgage.* With this type the initial cost is lower, because you start off at the lowest interest rate the bank, in order to meet competition from other lenders, dares offer today. But you agree to abide by regular review and escalation or de–escalation as interest rates are adjusted up or down by the lender to meet the conditions of the money market. Under strict government guidelines, the rates may change every month. The adjustment, however, is usually scheduled every six months or once a year, with the rate permitted to increase no more than a maximum of two percent a year. The rate changes are tied to a number of interest–based indices published by the federal government, and usually there is a "cap," or ceiling, beyond which the rate may not be raised, as well as a downward floor. In theory, however, there is no limit on how high or how low the rate may go over the life of the loan.

While the ARM interest rate is usually lower at first than that on a fixed–rate mortgage, the risk you take is that it will eventually equal it or even exceed it. If, on the other hand, the adjustable rate holds steady or goes down, you may come out ahead.

Under an ARM, the amount you have to pay to the bank could change every month or every six months as the rates change. With most ARMs, you sign up for a fixed monthly payment that will stay the same through a given period before an adjustment is made. If you are hit with an upward adjustment that is more than your budget can stand, see if the bank will keep the payments the same and extend the life of the loan. What the bank does is determine, based on the current interest rate, how much of your payment to apply to the principal that you borrowed and how much to pay interest at the current rate. If the interest rate goes down, the bank puts more of your payment toward paying back the principal. If the interest rate rises, on the other hand, the bank applies more and more of your payment to interest charges and less and less to paying off the principal. Conceivably, this could increase your debt: If the interest charge becomes higher than the total payment you are sending in each month, you get into what is called "negative amortization," actually increasing rather than "paying down" your loan. Let's look at an example.

Suppose you obtain an adjustable–rate mortgage for $45,000 for 30 years at 11.5 percent annual adjustment. Your monthly payment will be $445.64. In the second year, however, the interest rate rises to 12.5 percent. Now your payment *should* be $480.27—but you elect (and the bank allows you) to keep the payment the same. Thus, when each monthly check comes in from you, the bank first takes its payment of interest, at 12.5 percent, then applies anything left over to reducing your principal. As long as the rate of interest stays at 12.5 percent (or goes even higher) you will be falling further and further behind in the amount that is being applied toward your principal. For instance, with a payment of $445.64 at

11.5 percent, let's assume that $400 is for interest payment and the balance goes toward the principal. If you make the same payment at 12.5 percent, the payment going toward the interest will increase, let's say to $410, and thus less will go toward paying the principal. If, on the other hand, the interest rate should fall to 10.5 percent, which would call for a monthly payment of $411.64, and you continue to send in your fixed payment of $445.65, the bank will apply less of your payment to interest and more to reducing your principal balance—and you will be paying down your loan at a faster rate.

Tip: Some ARM's have no cap on the interest rate they may charge you. They can just go up and up. *Avoid them.*

The moral of all this is to try to find a bank that offers an ARM with infrequent adjustment and with a cap on increases in the interest rate or in monthly payments.

Some variations on the ARM that you should know about:

- *Graduated payment mortgage.* With this type of mortgage the monthly payments are relatively low in the first few years. Then they rise until they are higher than conventional monthly mortgage payments would be. The idea is that payments are scheduled to increase at fixed intervals and by fixed amounts. The problem is that the payments in the early years might not be covering the interest, so you are not building any equity in your home unless property values are increasing generally.
- *Renegotiable–rate mortgage.* With this type the interest rate comes up for renegotiation after a set period, usually one to five years, rather than when market factors, such as a change in the prime rate, force it to change. The new rate is determined, as is the adjustable rate, by the Federal Home Loan Bank Board.
- *Roll–over mortgage.* This is similar to the renegotiable–rate mortgage. The rate is set for from three to five years. Then it is totally

renegotiated, or "rolled over." In effect, the roll–over involves a series of short–term loans, with the entire loan coming due at the end of each period and then being replaced by another short–term loan. This goes on for a total of 25 or 30 years, as in conventional mortgages.
- *Balloon mortgage.* For the first few years, this one is similar to the variable, or adjustable–rate, mortgage, and you are paying it off like the conventional loan of 30 years. But at the end of a specified time, usually three to five years, you get hit with a "balloon" payment of the entire balance, which you pay by obtaining a new loan at the interest rates that then prevail. This type of loan is often used in second mortgages. If on the second time around, when the balloon is due, you can borrow at lower interest rates than you were able to get the first time, you have the advantage. This is not a sure thing, however, and, in addition, you could then be in an economic situation that makes borrowing difficult.
- *The assumable mortgage.* Sometimes you can assume the existing mortgage of the person who is selling the house. But you must come up with the difference between the asking price and the balance that is due on the mortgage. Suppose you are buying a $110,000 home on which the owner still owes $50,000 on the mortgage. If the owner's rate of interest is low, this could be an advantage for you, but now you will have to come up with $60,000. You may already have part of that amount as your planned down payment. To provide the missing difference, you could try to obtain a second mortgage. Or you might try making a deal with the bank that holds the previous owner's low–interest mortgage. They might be willing to make a "composite" loan—a new loan at a lower rate than is now prevailing, in order for them to "retire" the previous owner's loan, which has recently been giving them no profit margin at all.

Tip: Banks do negotiate. Banks do make deals. Banks do bend their own rules, if they see that you have a secure future. They will bend over backwards for a young doctor, or for someone who is going into a successful, closely held family business. When they know you are on a fast track, they anticipate future business—and they will negotiate. They will not, however, bend government rules. Don't expect them to. If you cannot get the loan you want and the amount you need, consider what is known as "creative financing." Many lending institutions will handle second mortgages. Often a seller, especially if he or she is anxious to close the deal, will finance part of the buyer's purchase price (a "take–back" mortgage). Many real estate developers offer special financing on new homes.

HOW MUCH OF A MORTGAGE CAN JEANNE AND ERIC TAKE ON?

They have a monthly gross income of $4,916—28 percent is $1,376. This is the most they can spend per month on their mortgage payment, taxes and insurance. But what would be their total debt–to–income ratio if they added their car and student loans to that mortgage figure—$1,376 plus $563 (two car loans and student loans, see their budget on page 75). It would be $1,939, which is higher than 36 percent of their gross income. Thirty–six percent of their income is $1,770. To keep within the total debt–to–income ratio, they will have to hold their mortgage debt at $1,207 or less.

Remember: Buying your home will probably be the largest and most important investment you will ever make. It's worth taking the time and trouble to check every aspect of your purchase and make the very best deal you can on the house and on the mortgage terms. Remember, too, that even if the price is high and the bank's interest rates are high, your home can be a valuable source of tax savings, capital growth, and protection against inflation. And if it works out right, owning a home often costs no more, or very little more, than renting.

Tax deductions and other savings.

What are some of those tax savings you gain as homeowners? Here are ways you can take deductions from your income tax:

1. *Mortgage interest.* The interest you pay to a lender on a mortgage loan is tax deductible, whether the mortgage is for a place that is for personal use (a place to live in), business use (a place to operate a business in), or income–producing use (a place you've bought as an investment, to rent to others). The interest you pay is deducted from your adjusted gross income. It may be claimed as an itemized deduction only on Schedule A, Form 1040.

   Your monthly mortgage payments cover interest on the principal amount you owe, plus repayment of some of the principal. In addition, some banks pay your real estate taxes and insurance for you and add that to the total, so you are paying one–twelfth of those costs each month. Most lending institutions provide you with a statement at the end of the year specifying how much you have paid during the year for each item.

   At the time of the closing on your mortgage, you may have to pay some "points." This is a one–time expense. Each point equals one percent of your mortgage ($450, for example, on a $45,000 mortgage). If points are considered to be prepaid interest, they are usually deductible on your income tax return. If they are considered a service fee, they are not deductible, so this is a question to ask when you are shopping for your mortgage. If the points are deductible, insist on paying for them with a separate check, so you have a record, rather than letting the bank automatically take them out of your loan.

2. *Real property taxes.* These are local taxes imposed on all property owners. They are deductible from your federal income tax. The money they bring in is, in most communities, the main revenue that pays for schools and roads and municipal services such as police and fire departments and refuse collection.

   Don't be surprised to find that taxes have a way of increasing as the value of property increases. Your city or town will reassess property every few years and increase taxes based on the new assessments. As mentioned earlier, this could happen soon after you move into your home, so before you buy find out what's going on in the locality where you are buying. Then at least you won't be surprised.

HOW THE NICHOLSES MADE THEIR DECISION...

Jeanne and Eric are doing a lot of paperwork before they make a bid on a house. They have gone to banks and checked on mortgage rates, then got application forms from the bank that seemed most likely to give them the best rate. These forms include questions on their employment and earnings, which the bank will verify. "Then we really worked on our finances," says Jeanne. "We want to be good and sure we can afford the house. And we've figured out a whole new budget that we'll have to follow if we actually own a house."

More preparations: They've asked the bank to figure out the dollar amount of the mortgage and its monthly payments (including the interest and the amount needed to pay both the local real estate taxes and homeowner's insurance annually, to be placed into what is called an escrow account). They rebudgeted all their expenses.

They reworked their budget and here's how some of the figures came out: The average monthly total expense of living in their apartment is $994.20 ($11,930 per year). They figure the new house will average $1,280 per month ($15,360 a year)—or $286 more per month than they are paying now (assuming a 30–year adjustable mortgage of $125,000 at 8.75 percent). On a yearly basis, however, the average will be considerably less, for now on their income tax return they will be able to deduct from their gross income the interest they will pay to the bank as well as their real estate taxes. The total Federal tax savings will be $3,376.

Your Home as an Investment

A home can be a valuable source of tax savings, inflation protection, and capital growth.

In many cases, the cost of buying a home isn't any higher than renting. Fill in the following information to determine the difference between owning and renting.

Owning (Annual Costs)

Home Expenses:		Income Tax Deductions:	
Real Estate Taxes	$ _1,200_	Real Estate Taxes	$ _1,200_
Mortgage Interest	$ _10,860_	Mortgage Interest	$ _10,860_
Mortgage Principal	$ _950_	**Subtotal II**	$ _12,060_
Homeowner's Insurance	$ _360_	**Your Income Tax Bracket:**	
Repairs	$ _500_	State	_____%
Utilities	$ _1,500_	Federal	_28_%
Subtotal I	$ _15,370_	**Subtotal III**	_28_%

- Multiply your income tax deductions (II) by your personal tax rate (III) to discover your total tax savings (IV).

$$ \$ \underset{\text{II}}{\underline{12,060}} \times \underset{\text{III}}{\underline{28}} = \$ \underset{\text{IV}}{\underline{3,376}} $$

- Subtract your total tax savings (IV) from your total home expenses (I) to find the cost of owning your home after taxes (this figure does not include the value of appreciation of your home).

$$ \$ \underset{\text{I}}{\underline{15,370}} - \$ \underset{\text{IV}}{\underline{3,376}} = \$ \underset{\text{V}}{\underline{11,994}} \quad \textbf{Total Cost of Owning Your Home} $$

RENTING (Annual Costs)

Rent	$ _11,000_	
Renter's Insurance	$ _110_	
Utilities	$ _720_	
	$ _11,830_ (VI)	**Total Cost of Renting**

- Subtract Total Cost of Renting (VI) From Total Cost of Owning (V).

$$ \$11,830 - \$11,994 = (\$164) $$

Your Home as an Investment

A home can be a valuable source of tax savings, inflation protection, and capital growth.

In many cases, the cost of buying a home isn't any higher than renting. Fill in the following information to determine the difference between owning and renting.

Owning (Annual Costs)

Home Expenses:		Income Tax Deductions:	
Real Estate Taxes	$ _____	Real Estate Taxes	$ _____
Mortgage Interest	$ _____	Mortgage Interest	$ _____
Mortgage Principal	$ _____	**Subtotal II**	$ _____
Homeowner's Insurance	$ _____	**Your Income Tax Bracket:**	
Repairs	$ _____	State	_____%
Utilities	$ _____	Federal	_____%
Subtotal I	$ _____	**Subtotal III**	_____%

- Multiply your income tax deductions (II) by your personal tax rate (III) to discover your total tax savings (IV).

$$\$ \underline{\hspace{4cm}} \times \underline{\hspace{4cm}} = \$ \underline{\hspace{4cm}}$$
$$\qquad\text{II}\qquad\qquad\qquad\text{III}\qquad\qquad\qquad\text{IV}$$

- Subtract your total tax savings (IV) from your total home expenses (I) to find the cost of owning your home after taxes (this figure does not include the value of appreciation of your home).

$$\$ \underline{\hspace{2cm}} - \$ \underline{\hspace{2cm}} = \$ \underline{\hspace{4cm}} \textbf{Total Cost of Owning Your Home}$$
$$\quad\text{I}\qquad\qquad\text{IV}\qquad\qquad\text{V}$$

RENTING (Annual Costs)

Rent	$ _____
Renter's Insurance	$ _____
Utilities	$ _____
	$ _____ **Total Cost of Renting**
	VI

- Subtract Total Cost of Renting (VI) From Total Cost of Owning (V).

INSURANCE: HOW MUCH DO YOU NEED? WHAT KIND SHOULD YOU GET?

11

I have to admit that I never knew much about insurance—*any* kind of insurance—until long after I was grown and married. When I was in high school, I put a few dents in the family car. I couldn't understand why my parents weren't paid the entire cost of repairs by the insurance company. When I was in college, my stereo was stolen. I fully expected my folks to collect the total cost of replacement from the insurance company.

Eventually I learned about the principles of insurance—how the idea is to spread the risk, with insurance premiums paid by a large number of people who are exposed to similar risks...how "deductibles" save the insurance company (and thus all those who are sharing the risks) the costs of paying countless very small claims that could eat up the reserves needed to pay more substantial claims.

Insurance covers many risks: the chance that someone will die and a productive source of income will disappear...the chance that something may be stolen or accidentally destroyed...the chance that health will fail and medical bills will have to be paid...the chance that someone will hold you responsible for personal injury or damage to property...the chance that fire will damage or destroy property, or will kill or injure people.

You now probably find yourselves thinking about insurance—all kinds of insurance—in a way you hadn't thought about it before. Until now, you may have had an "if anything happens, well, it won't matter all that much" attitude toward life insurance or even toward fire and theft and liability insurance. But now you find yourselves concerned about what the effect of loss, disability, or death would be on the other person.

The following discussion will cover all kinds of insurance and how they work. You must then decide on what insurance you need—and how much—for yourselves, your family, your situation. Let's start with the most important kind: life insurance.

Protecting income

The main purpose of life insurance is to protect the income part of your budget. Life insurance exists to replace the income that stops if the earner dies. But it does have another purpose: to accumulate savings.

The key word in thinking about life insurance is *now*. Now is not 10 years from today, and it is not last year. Yet countless people carry life insurance that was right last year or will be right 10 years from now. The fact is that as your life changes your insurance needs will change. It is important, in planning life insurance, to make it fit what you need *now*—maybe even more important than making it fit what you will need at some time in the future.

This does not mean you need to revise your life insurance coverage every year. But do be sure to review your needs and your coverage at least every five years. Otherwise you could be wasting money on insurance—or not buying enough.

The basic types of life insurance

The insurance world is loaded—in fact, it is over-loaded—with variations on types of policies. It seems as if every insurance company has its own. But all fall into one of four basic types:

1. *Term insurance.* As the name implies, this means you are buying life insurance for a specific term or period of time—usually one to five years. This is low–cost insurance. In fact, term is the cheapest form of life insurance you can buy. It pays off if you die. But it does not build up any savings or other benefits. It provides nothing but protection. When the term ends, you have nothing—but during the term you have been protected. If you renew for

another term, the cost is higher because you are older and the likelihood of death is greater as you get older. If you keep buying term insurance, you will find that by the age of 45 or 50 the premium cost is rising rapidly—much faster than in earlier years—and it is no longer "low-cost" insurance. But by the time you reach that age, you should not be buying term anyway, or you certainly should be buying less of it.

Term insurance is really ideal for a young couple. It gives you greater amounts of protection at less cost than whole or straight life insurance.

> *Tip:* If you are buying term, be sure the policy you get can be renewed without your having to pass another physical examination. Also be sure it contains a clause that permits you to convert it into a whole policy without a physical— and at a guaranteed rate. These factors— renewability and convertibility—can be vitally important if your health changes during the term and you become uninsurable or become a high risk, which would send the cost of a policy up to a prohibitive rate.

2. *Whole– or straight–life insurance.* With this type, you get more than protection. You build up savings. At the time you buy the policy, the insurance company determines the amount of the premium by your age and state of health. The premium then stays the same as long as you keep the policy in force. Therefore, the younger you are when you buy a whole or straight policy, the less it costs you. During the first few years, the insurance company credits only a small amount of your total premium payments to savings. Then, as time goes on, the savings build up. This amount is yours if you cancel the policy. Or you can borrow the amount that is in savings, paying interest on it (at an interest rate you will find stated in your policy) to the insurance company. When you "borrow against the policy," you continue to pay the premium, keeping the policy in force. However, if you die, the insurance company deducts the amount you borrowed

from the "face amount" of the policy before it pays your beneficiary. For example, if you are buying a $25,000 policy but have borrowed $8,000 on it, the company will pay only $17,000.

This "policy loan" provision is a valuable right. It enables you to draw upon the "cash value" that has built up in your policy in order to meet financial needs.

3. *Endowment policy.* This is the ultimate in savings types of life insurance. It states a designated sum that will accumulate from the premiums you pay and the dividends the insurance company will pay. When the policy matures at the end of its specified period (say, 20 years, in a "20-year endowment policy"), the face amount is paid to the beneficiary you have named. If that beneficiary is no longer living, it goes to your contingent beneficiary, if you named one in your will. If you did not, it goes into your estate. The premium amount stays the same for the life of the policy.

4. *Universal life.* This is a variation of a whole–life insurance policy with a tax–deferred investment program that earns interest at money market rates. When you set up the policy with the insurance company, you decide how much of the premium you want to go toward buying insurance protection and how much you want put into investments. You may vary your annual death benefit and annual premium. In some years you might put more money toward the policy, thus building up cash values more quickly. In other years, you might want to put in less.

5. *Variable life.* One portion of the premium pays for insurance protection and the other—the investment portion—is invested according to your wishes. Thus, the money may be invested in stocks, bonds, mutual funds or zero coupon bonds. The insurance company manages the funds your investments are in, so you must choose from the investments that the company offers. But you may switch from one type of investment to another. This type of policy is for those who understand investments and feel comfortable with them.

6. *Single premium life.* The premium is made in one single lump sum, usually with a $5,000 minimum. As cash values build up, tax on them is deferred. You may borrow from the policy at any time. However, many companies impose a back–end load—that is, a charge if you make withdrawals during a certain period.

Which type of policy to buy?

You have to weigh the advantages and disadvantages of each kind of policy. The first question to ask yourself is: How much coverage do we really need right now? The second question: How much can we afford? If you are depending on both your incomes to maintain the household, think about near possibilities, too—such as what would happen if one of you died soon after you started a family. Tough question. But one you have to think about seriously. How much insurance would be needed by the spouse and child who were left?

Tip: When you are considering life insurance policies, weigh whether you are being sold on a whole- or straight-life policy, which costs more, when what you really need is a larger amount of protection, which you could buy for the same price by taking a term policy. If youth is on your side, you can buy a lot more insurance for a few years when you need the protection by buying term. Just don't keep term going for too many years, because it will cost more and more.

If you expect to keep a term policy for some years, look at what the total premiums will be for that period of time. Don't just look at the first year's cost, because prices for term insurance rise as you get older. Compare the cost per $1,000 of death benefits. The rates will depend on your age, sex, and health status and amount of coverage you want.

A key point to remember about whole life insurance is that the policy with the lowest premium may not be the best choice. Premiums are only one factor in building cash value. The others are investment results, interest–rate guarantees, fees and charges for mortality risk, commissions and favorable borrowing rules.

How to decide how much you need

Your insurance proceeds, invested at a reasonable rate of interest, should generate the income your beneficiaries need to fill the gap between their other financial resources and their financial need.

You should never buy any more life insurance than you need. How do you know how much you need? Worksheets are the only way. You can calculate exactly what's needed on Worksheet IX, filling in some of the information from the other worksheets you've already completed. Look at your budget worksheets. What income will be available to your spouse if you die? Here are the possibilities:

- Spouse's income, if he or she works or can return to work.
- Social Security payments, if the spouse is eligible for them.

A surviving spouse is eligible for benefits only if there are children under 16 and only as long as the spouse does not remarry.

Note: You should know what you are getting for those Social Security payments they deduct from your paycheck. It takes 10 years for you to become "fully insured" in the eyes of Social Security so that you are entitled to all its benefits in your retirement years. However, if a breadwinner has paid in during a total of six quarters, during any three calendar years before death, then he or she is "currently insured" and entitled to death benefits.

- Dividends and interest from investments (see Worksheet IV, **Sources of Income**).
- Benefits from a pension plan.
- Proceeds from insurance you already have in force or included in coverage where you work.

Next, look at the expense side of your budget. If you die, which expenses will decrease for your spouse and family? Probably food, clothing, transportation and life insurance premiums. The rule of thumb is 75 percent: Figure that a family in which either parent dies still needs at least three–quarters of its previous take–home pay in order to cover expenses and maintain its lifestyle. Imagine how tough it would be to plan insurance needs accurately if you did not have a good picture of what it costs you to live!

It's important to figure out the cash that would be needed, and that insurance should cover, if the bread-winner (or *either* breadwinner) died. Some of this necessary amount you have already listed on your Net Worth Statement. Be sure to include:

- Current debts (unpaid bills as well as installment loans and mortgage).
- Expected education expenses. If you already have children, it's important (no matter how young they are) to know what it is going to cost to educate them. When you receive the proceeds from a life insurance policy, earmark enough for college, and invest it at a rate of return that would keep up with the ever–increasing costs of college.
- Final expenses that a death brings. These include administration of the estate, probate costs, attorney's and accountant's fees, appraisal fees, taxes, final medical expenses that are not reimbursed from major medical or other insurance plans, and funeral expenses. Allow 2 to 5 percent of the total estate, plus up to $5,000 for funeral expenses, to cover these.

With so many variables, you can see how the amount of insurance you need can change as life changes. When you're buying a home and raising your children, your needs keep increasing. When the mortgage is paid off and the children finish college, your needs decrease. At least once every five years, look over your needs and the insurance you have been buying to cope with them. And remember that Financial Fitness does not demand that you be over–insured. Plan carefully and buy the amount of coverage you need—not the amount an agent wants to sell you. To help guide you, your net worth statement and budget worksheets will tell you which assets will produce income, which liabilities should be paid off with proceeds from life insurance, and what it will cost either of you to maintain your lifestyle if you lose your spouse.

Tip: Many young couples figure bad news is something that always happens to someone else. Let me urge you to be hardheaded and practical—but certainly not morbid—in your thinking. I can promise you that, once you have gone through this tough thinking and made sensible plans that are workable for your situation, you will be able to feel relaxed about the future.

What happens if an insured person dies?

There are several ways, called *settlement options*, in which an insurance company pays out the policy after the death of the insured person. When you are buying the policy, the agent may try to get you to pick one of these options so it can be specified in the policy. You do not have to decide then, however, and in fact it is unfair to ask you to decide then because it is impossible for you to know, when the policy is created, what will best serve your family's needs some time in the future. A few intervening years can change too many things. If you are pressured to decide among the options, hold your ground firmly.

Pressure can also come immediately after the death of the insured person. If you are the beneficiary, the insurance company is likely to ask you for a decision right away, but you can ask them to hold the proceeds of the policy until you have had time to weigh the options. Take your time, and don't let anyone rush you into it or make the decision for you. The options are:

1. *Lump sum.* This means you get a check immediately for the full amount of the policy (less any amount that may have been borrowed out). If you are into investments and are already knowledgeable about them (or if you have good advice and are willing to learn), this can be a good option. If interest rates are running high, you should be able to get a better return on investment than the insurance company can provide.
2. *Interest only.* This means the insurance company holds the principal amount but pays you the interest it is earning—a good holding position while you decide what to do with the proceeds.
3. *Fixed installments.* Here, the insurance company agrees to pay you a fixed amount at regular intervals, until the money is all gone. Meantime, it also pays interest on the remaining balance it is holding.
4. *Fixed period.* The company sets a period of time over which it will pay out the proceeds, plus accrued interest. The size of each check depends on how long a time you choose to have the proceeds spread over.

Tips:
- If you choose the fixed installment or fixed period, be sure you have the right to change your mind and withdraw the entire sum at a later date.
- If you are going to buy an annuity (an investment the purpose of which is to pay you a fixed income for a fixed number of years) you do not *have* to buy the annuity through the insurance company. Check what the company offers and compare it with other annuity contracts. Get the highest monthly income possible for each $1,000 you have available to set up the annuity.
- If you have a mortgage, be cautious about paying it off. Even if the proceeds from an insurance policy make it possible to pay off a mortgage, that may not be the best thing to do. For instance, you might be able to take the money you would use to pay it off and invest it at higher rates of interest.

Practical details of life insurance policies

A life insurance policy is a legal contract. Every policy has three parts:

1. *The summary.* This contains the essential details of what you and the insurance company have agreed between you. You agree to pay a stipulated premium on a regular basis. The premium is based on your age and condition of health. In return for your paying the premium, the company agrees to pay the face amount (less any loans that have been made to you, if it is a whole- or straight-life policy), provided the policy is in force at the time of your death. Usually two additions are made to the summary, if you elect to have them: a) waiver of premium, which means that if you become permanently disabled and unable to earn income the company will continue the policy without your paying for it, and b) an accidental–death "rider" by which the company usually doubles the face value of the policy (e.g., if you are insured for $10,000 and die as the result of an accident, the company pays $20,000 to your beneficiary).

2. *The details*. This is the nitty–gritty: the date your premium payments will be due (you choose from quarterly, semiannual, or annual payments); the grace period (how long you are allowed to go without paying the premium before a penalty will be imposed or the policy canceled—usually 31 days); lapses (how soon the policy will expire if you don't pay); non–forfeiture surrender values (the money you would have coming, under a cash surrender policy, for instance, if you decided to give up the policy or if you simply let it lapse by not paying for it); extended term and reduced paid–up options (ways you can use the cash values that have built up in your policy to provide continuing coverage without making any further payments); and settlement options (as already described in this chapter).

3. *The application*. This is the application form you fill out in order to get the policy. It lists your age, health, other life insurance policies you have, your occupation and activities that may or may not be considered dangerous to your life and health, and how you wish to exercise the rights you have under the policy, such as changing the designation of beneficiary at a later date.

What about life insurance for women?

For many generations, life insurance has been sold mostly to cover the male breadwinner. But today, with more than half of married American women working at full-time jobs and with more and more single parents, there are many women who should have life insurance.

Any couple or family that depends on two incomes to maintain its lifestyle ought to have life insurance on both the man and the woman. If there are children, this is even more important. Insurance should be provided so a husband can gain some replacement for the wife's income, and vice versa, and so the burden of taking care of children is covered during their young years. Often a group insurance program where either of the couple works can cover immediate cash requirements, but does not replace income.

Any single person who has been married and is responsible for supporting children simply *must* have life insurance that will provide coverage until the children are no longer dependent.

How about the spouse—woman or man—who has given up a job to be the homemaker? She—or he—provides services that would cost dollars and cents, and plenty of them, if household help had to be hired for cooking, cleaning, child care, gardening, decorating, chauffeuring. In addition to calculating the values of all those services, you might figure in the expenses of a major illness and, needless to say, of a funeral when you contemplate life insurance on a helpmate.

To find out how much insurance is needed to replace a homemaker, look at both immediate and future needs. Immediate involves the costs of settling the estate and paying for the funeral. Future includes housekeeping and child care for a number of years. To arrive at a sensible figure, work out the monthly cost in dollars, multiply by 12 months and then by the number of years before the children will be on their own.

Insurance on business partners

If one of you is an entrepreneur or has a small business with one or two partners, life insurance is a must. Probably the business is the largest asset you have. It needs protecting so it will continue if a partner or major shareholder dies.

Life insurance can provide the funds for the surviving members of the business to purchase the share owned by the partner who died, thus saving the widow or widower from the nightmare of trying to take up where the deceased spouse left off, and saving the partners from the difficulty of coping with the surviving spouse's coming into the business—and from the embarrassment of not having enough money to buy this person out.

How much insurance is needed? Enough to equal the partner's or shareholder's interest in the business. The arrangement should be formalized in a buy–sell agreement among the partners.

If you are a single owner of a business, life insurance can give your widow or widower the money to live on while the business is being liquidated—again, avoiding the complications of taking over a business that one may not understand or want to be in, but which provides one's livelihood.

Some key points about life insurance

There are some simple steps to take:

1. Do your homework. Know what you want to buy and the amount you want to buy before you start pricing individual policies.
2. Buy whole or straight life, or cash value, insurance if you want the premium to stay the same and if you want to build up savings.
3. Buy term insurance if you want maximum protection for the amount you can afford to spend on insurance now and in the immediate future.
4. Shop around. Costs and policy terms vary from company to company. Ask friends and business associates for the names of agents with whom they were satisfied.
5. If possible, take advantage of group insurance. It costs less than an individual policy. Check where you work.
6. Remember that your life insurance program should not be carved in stone. Review it regularly—at least once every five years. Recalculate income versus expenses and decide for yourself whether you need to increase or decrease your coverage. Always match coverage to realistic needs.
7. Be aware of the long–term effects of inflation. Insurance you buy based on today's dollars will be worth less and less in purchasing power. So try to think ahead and budget an amount for life insurance that is the best balance you can reach between what you can afford today and what you might need over the next five years.
8. Don't be rushed into signing. If you don't understand, ask the agent to explain a policy's provisions.
9. Consider some of the specialized forms of life insurance, such as:

    a. *Mortgage life insurance.* Insurance companies and banks sell policies (usually it's a *decreasing term policy*) to cover the portion of a mortgage that would still be owed if the homeowner died at any time. In decreasing term insurance, the premiums remain the same each year but the amount that would be paid in the event of a claim declines each year as the mortgage is paid off. In most cases, the lending institution that holds the mortgage is listed as the beneficiary and is paid directly by the insurance company if there is a claim. My own recommendation: It's better to consider *all* your insurance needs carefully and on balance, and include enough protection to cover your unpaid mortgage. In fact, in many cases it is not even a good idea to pay off the mortgage if its interest rate is a reasonable one. That big a lump of money might be better used for other purposes.

    b. *Credit life insurance.* This is like mortgage insurance, but covers such consumer credit as a loan to buy a car. Sometimes the insurance is built into the loan and you get it whether you want it or not. The premium is added to the loan and financed at the same rate, so you end up paying to insure not only the loan principal but also the insurance premium and all the finance charges. In effect—and in actuality—you are insuring the insurance. Incidentally, it is usually legal for a creditor to require you to have insurance as security for the debt. State laws generally make it illegal, however, for creditors to require you to buy it from them. Chances are it will be much cheaper to buy it elsewhere, and you may also be able to pledge a policy you already have. If you cannot meet the health requirements for other insurance coverage, credit life could be a reasonable way to get some protection. Generally, it is better to include coverage for outstanding credit in your total insurance needs. Credit is a liability, remember. You should figure on having a way to cover it in your insurance.

NOW THAT THEY HAVE A HOUSE AND CHILDREN...

...the Bucks realize they must have extra life and disability insurance. Pat's company provides $120,000 of term insurance, and he has another $100,000 term policy that he bought soon after Landon was born. Karen's company provides a $55,000 policy.

Since there are children under 16, Karen or Pat would receive Social Security benefits if one or the other died. Landon and Megan would also receive benefits until each is age 18 (19 if they are full–time students). However, Karen's survivors would receive less in Social Security benefits than Pat's because her average annual earnings have been less than his. In addition to Social Security, there would be the survivor's income and income from the proceeds of existing life insurance policies. This would cover their basic living expenses.

But they've talked it over, and both realize that they need more insurance to cover the mortgage and the future educational expenses for the children. If the worst happened—if Pat died—Karen could pay off the mortgage or invest the insurance money to provide the income necessary to make the monthly payments.

Karen and Pat plan to review their insurance needs every few years. They know that their basic expenses will keep going up with inflation, and having enough life insurance will help the survivor to maintain the standard of living they are used to.

Disability insurance

What happens if either of you is disabled by an accident or an illness? The odds that you will be disabled for an extended period before you reach 65 are greater than the odds that you will die before then. If you are disabled, chances are highly likely for your income to drop and your medical bills to climb—simultaneously. That would be disastrous. So whether you are male or female, if your ability to produce income is vital to your situation, you must have insurance that will replace that income if a period of disability stops it. Only a small percentage of American workers are covered by disability insurance.

Social Security provides disability insurance for those who become severely disabled before they reach 65. It is important to know that seven out of 10 disability claims filed under Social Security are rejected. It considers you to be disabled if you have a physical or mental condition so severe it prevents you from working and is expected to last (or has

already lasted) for at least 12 months, or if it is expected to result in death. You have to wait five months after your disability begins before Social Security starts to pay. It pays the same amount as you would start to get upon your retirement at age 65. To be eligible, you must be fully insured under the Social Security regulations (that is, you must have worked for 40 quarter–years or 10 full years).

Disability insurance as a fringe benefit

Most employers these days provide some sort of disability insurance. Probably either or both of you are covered by one of these two types of plan:

1. *Short–term.* This provides modest benefits for a short period. It usually pays weekly, based on your earnings, but with a maximum that can be as low as $150 a week. The waiting period before it starts to pay is from seven to 21 days (i.e., you must be disabled that long before you can start to collect). Some plans pay only for as few as 13 weeks. Others pay for as long as 52 weeks.
2. *Long–term.* This plan is designed to take care of more serious disabilities. Most plans provide a certain percentage of earnings (probably 50 or 60 percent of your base salary). The maximum monthly payment may be $1,500 or $2,000, or more; the waiting period may be anywhere from three to six months; and the payments may continue (if you continue to be disabled) any number of years (5, 10, or 20), or until you reach 65. The fact is, there is a wide variety of benefits and conditions, because there are almost as many different disability policies as there are employers. Check what your company or both your companies are offering and participate in the one that gives you the best plan.

Why does everything seem to stop at age 65? Because that's when Social Security and Medicare take over. Since these two government programs are so universal, and since most people have traditionally retired at 65, the insurance companies just don't bother to work out actuarial tables or develop premium rates for employee group insurance after 65. However, any number of insurance companies do offer individual policies. Many advertise that they

Worksheet X: Pat Buck
HOW MUCH LIFE INSURANCE?

A. ANNUAL FAMILY LIVING COSTS, without mortgage
(from Budget form).   _45,000_

B. SOURCES OF INCOME AVAILABLE

● Spouse's Income _____ 28,000 _____

● Social Security Benefits _____ 21,600 _____

● Income from Income-Producing
Assets (from Budget form) _____ 1,000 _____

● Income from Proceeds of Existing Life Insurance Policies
(use an assumed rate of interest)

6%—multiply amount of insurance by .06
10%—multiply amount of insurance by .10
12%—multiply amount of insurance by .12

_220,000_ × .10 = _22,000_

● Other Sources of Income _____

TOTAL SOURCES OF INCOME   _72,600_

C. ADDITIONAL INCOME NEEDED (subtract B from A)   _(27,600)_

D. AMOUNT OF MONEY TO MAKE UP SHORTAGE
(at an assumed rate of interest)
6%—divide by .06
10%—divide by .10
12%—divide by .12

_____ ÷ .10   _____

E. ADDITIONAL CASH REQUIREMENTS

Final Expenses _____ 10,000 _____

Education for Children _____ 47,060 (both children) _____

Liabilities (including Mortgage) _____ 216,500 _____   _273,560_

F. INSURANCE NEEDS (D plus E)   _245,960_

Worksheet X: Karen Buck
HOW MUCH LIFE INSURANCE?

A. ANNUAL FAMILY LIVING COSTS, without mortgage
(from Budget form)   _45,000_

B. SOURCES OF INCOME AVAILABLE

● Spouse's Income ____61,500____

● Social Security Benefits ____15,600____

● Income from Income-Producing
Assets (from Budget form) ____1,000____

● Income from Proceeds of Existing Life Insurance Policies
(use an assumed rate of interest)

6%—multiply amount of insurance by .06
10%—multiply amount of insurance by .10
12%—multiply amount of insurance by .12

____55,000____ × .10 = _5,500_

● Other Sources of Income _____

TOTAL SOURCES OF INCOME   _83,600_

C. ADDITIONAL INCOME NEEDED (subtract B from A)   _(38,600)_

D. AMOUNT OF MONEY TO MAKE UP SHORTAGE
(at an assumed rate of interest)
6%—divide by .06
10%—divide by .10
12%—divide by .12

_____ ÷ .10   _____

E. ADDITIONAL CASH REQUIREMENTS

Final Expenses ____10,000____

Education for Children ____47,060 (both children)____

Liabilities (including Mortgage) ____216,500____   _273,560_

F. INSURANCE NEEDS (D plus E)   _234,960_ pay a certain flat amount daily, unrelated to any medical bills or hospital costs, "from the first day of hospitalization." Such policies are carried by many people who are over 65. They are, in effect, simple disability policies.

Importance of individual policy

Since Social Security and group plans do not usually pay as much as you really need if you become disabled, it could be important for you to have an individual disability policy. If you buy one, the insurance company will base your premium on your age, condition of health, occupation, and income. Policies vary widely, so be sure you know what you are buying.

Features that affect your coverage include:

- Maximum benefit period. The length of time during which the company will pay. Usually expressed in weeks, months, or years. Some policies run for a lifetime as long as you pay the premiums.
- Perils insured against. Either accident only or accident and illness. Be sure you get coverage for both. Some policies that shout their bargain rates in advertising are accident–only, and will not pay you one cent if you are disabled as a result of illness.
- Elimination period. The time that must elapse, after your disability begins, before the company starts to pay. Usually 30, 60, 90, or 120 days. In some policies, even longer.
- Definition of disability. The conditions under which you will be considered disabled for the purpose of collecting benefits.

In buying any disability policy, make sure:

1. The insurance company cannot cancel, increase the premium, or alter the benefits during the life of the policy.
2. The policy is guaranteed renewable.
3. The period covered makes sense. It may be as short as one year or as long as until you reach 65, or your entire lifetime. The longer the coverage, the higher the premium you'll pay.
4. When benefits start. The longer the elimination period before payments begin, the lower your premium. Polices that pay out early (soon after

you are disabled) usually charge disproportionately high premiums.
5. A Future Income Option should be added to the policy. This will allow you to purchase additional coverage as your income increases—without your providing any evidence of medical insurability.

How much disability insurance do you need—and can you afford?

Go back to your worksheets—especially budget and net worth statement. Use Worksheet X to calculate what it costs you to live and what sources of income you would continue to have if you become disabled. Look over your current expenses—and then remember that you can be sure expenses will *rise* if you are disabled. If you should have the bad luck to need special medical provisions and special cares, expenses will go up like a rocket.

WHAT IF KAREN OR PAT BUCK WERE DISABLED?

Equally important is disability insurance for both of them. Pat's company provides some short-term insurance, but Karen's does not. Since they know that 70 percent of those who apply for Social Security disability benefits do not get them, they did not include Social Security disability benefits in calculating their need for disability insurance.

Health insurance

Let's face it: A major illness can dump staggering bills on you. Medical costs have not just gone sky–high in recent years—they've reached outer space. So it is essential for you to understand the various types of health insurance you can get, and how to file claims and get the coverage you are entitled to. If at all possible, you should be covered by a group plan, to cut down costs.

It is equally important to keep up to date on the subject. Review your medical insurance regularly every couple of years, and more often as circumstan-

Worksheet XI: Pat Buck
HOW MUCH DISABILITY INSURANCE?

A. ANNUAL FAMILY EXPENSES _____67,000_____

B. SOURCES OF INCOME

• Spouse's Net Income __21,000_____

• Social Security Benefits_____

• Disability Benefits from Work __24,000_____

Income from Income-Producing Assets
(Assets Evaluation form) _____1,000_____

• Other Income_____

TOTAL SOURCES OF INCOME _____46,000_____

C. ADDITIONAL ANNUAL INCOME NEEDED
(Subtract B from A) _____21,000_____

D. MONTHLY BENEFIT NEEDED _____1,750_____

---

ces change: children are born, grown children leave home, you move or are relocated by your company or change jobs.

If you are covered under a group plan where you work, the personnel office there should be able to help you understand exactly what coverage you are getting. If not, you will have to depend on an insurance broker (who handles policies from many companies and knows the advantages and disadvantages of each) or an insurance agent (who represents only a single company) to explain the facts. Listen carefully. Don't hesitate to ask questions, even if you think you're going to sound dumb or naive. If you find there are gaps in your coverage, ask how to close them, how much it will cost, whether or not it is worth it.

Read any policy carefully. Be sure you understand all the small print. You may hear an agent explain that

a particular policy will pay up to $25,000 on your surgical bills. In the small print, however, you may discover that $25,000 is the most the insurance company will pay in your entire lifetime. Quite a difference.

1. *Basic hospitalization.* This is provided by private insurance companies and the various Blue Cross policies nationwide. The policy usually pays all or part of a person's hospital bills, including a semi–private room, food, X rays, laboratory tests, operating room fees, and drugs. Usually there is a limit on the number of days the patient may spend in the hospital during any one illness, with a waiting period (usually 90 days) between stays. The better the coverage, the more it costs.

Worksheet XI: Karen Buck
HOW MUCH DISABILITY INSURANCE?

A. ANNUAL FAMILY EXPENSES

_67,000_

B. SOURCES OF INCOME

• Spouse's Net Income _50,000_

• Social Security Benefits _____

• Disability Benefits from Work _____

Income from Income-Producing Assets
(Assets Evaluation form) _1,000_

• Other Income_____

TOTAL SOURCES OF INCOME

_51,000_

C. ADDITIONAL ANNUAL INCOME NEEDED
(Subtract B from A)

_16,000_

D. MONTHLY BENEFIT NEEDED

_1,333_

2. *Basic surgical and medical expense.* Again, private companies provide these policies, although the nationwide Blue Shield (usually associated with Blue Cross) is best known. Fees for surgeons or other physicians are paid separately from hospital fees. Usually the insurance company sets a "schedule" of certain fees that it is willing to pay for certain operations. If your surgeon charges more than that fee, you must pay the difference yourself. Obviously, again, the better the coverage the more it costs.

Note: Often, basic hospitalization is combined with basic medical–surgical coverage, as in the Blue Cross/Blue Shield plans. Everyone should have at least this basic coverage.

3. *Major Medical.* This type of policy starts where basic hospitalization and basic medical/surgical insurance leave off. It covers the big expenses that are above the maximums of those policies. Usually a Major Medical policy covers extensive hospitalization, surgery, other doctors' fees, private–duty nursing, home medical care, diagnostic work, therapies, medical devices, and rehabilitation. Major Medical policies contain a deductible feature, so you pay a certain amount (usually from $100 to $1,000) before the insurance company pays anything. (Often, the deductible is annual: With each new year, you pay the first $100 or so of claims

yourself before the insurance company pays anything.) Once you have gone beyond the deductible amount, most Major Medical policies pay 80 percent or 85 percent of each claim you file. This is called "co–insurance." Usually if you are paying 15 or 20 percent in co–insurance, it goes up to a point—called the "stop–loss limit" and usually set at $2,000 or so—at which the company takes over and pays 100 percent of all legitimate claims. Even this, however, may have a top lifetime limit or maximum. It can be anywhere from $250,000 to $500,000—or entirely limitless. So read the policy and know where you stand.

Tips: If you are shopping for a Major Medical policy (that is, if you have a choice, rather than having to accept whatever your company's personnel department has set up), consider:

1. How much is the deductible? Is it per person covered or per family? (Some policies have a $100 deductible on you, and another $100 deductible on your spouse.)
2. Is the deductible per year—or per claim?
3. What expenses can be applied toward the deductible?
4. What is the maximum the insurance company will pay after you have met the deductible requirements?
5. How much is your co–insurance requirement then?
6. What is the stop–loss limit?
7. What is the absolute maximum the insurance company will pay?
8. Is the policy guaranteed to be renewable (i.e., does the company guarantee that you can keep on renewing it no matter what your state of health)? How long? To what age?
9. Just what limitations does the policy have?

If you are both working, you can each—theoretically—be cited as a dependent on the other's policy. But something called "coordination of benefits" enters into the situation. It usually prevents you both from collecting claims on both policies. One insurance company will make its policy the "primary carrier" on you, with the other insurance company the secondary carrier. Check with each of your personnel departments. Discuss coordination of benefits, and make sure you understand where you stand (you want to avoid getting into a situation like two outfielders who each think the other is about to catch the ball). Many employers, recognizing the situation of couples who are both employed and are offered similar benefits, will permit one of you to drop the Major Medical coverage and pick up something else instead—maybe a dental plan that you couldn't otherwise get. This option is called "cafeteria" benefits or a "cafeteria" plan. (See Chapter 9.)

Example: Suppose you have a Major Medical plan with an annual deductible of $100 and a stop–loss limit of $2,000. If you have an illness that brings a $1,800 claim, you will have to pay $340 out of your own pocket:

Total claim	$1,800
Less deductible	-100
	$1,700
Insurance co. pays	
80 percent	-1,360
You pay	$340

Once your out–of–pocket expenses reach $2,000, the insurance company will pick up 100 percent of the medical bill. Your out–of–pocket expenses are calculated to include the $100 deductible as well as all the 15 to 20 percent co–insurance that you have paid.

Any way you can cut down on the cost of a major–medical policy? Yes.

1. Increase the deductible. This means you assume more of the routine medical costs and the insurance company reduces its share of the risk that you will have really large medical bills.
2. Ask for a higher stop–lost limit.

Either step increases the risk you are willing to take on. What you have to do is decide how much risk you can afford to shoulder. Many people would rather pay a higher premium and not have to worry that the out–of–pocket expenses, if a major illness occurs, will send them to the bank to borrow money.

Some things to look for in health insurance

- Combination plans. Many companies, as well as Blue Cross/Blue Shield, offer plans that combine basic hospitalization and medical and surgical benefits with a major–medical plan. This package deal often has lower deductibles.
- Items that are not covered. Check on coverage for cosmetic surgery, eyeglasses and routine checkups for glasses, regular routine physicals and psychiatric care (if covered, psychiatric care is usually under some special limitation).
- Guaranteed renewable and non–cancelable policies. Some companies reserve the right to cancel at any time. This could be disastrous if they canceled some day after you had become uninsurable, or when you have an illness that existed before they canceled. A non–cancelable policy cannot be canceled during the period it is stated to run. Nor can premiums be increased during this period. Usually, when the stated period has ended (and it can be as short as one year), the company must renew the policy if the policyholder chooses to have it renewed. The company may, however, increase the premium.
- Shop around and consider the alternatives. Everyone should have Major Medical insurance. A major illness or accident can cause severe economic chaos. If you are eligible for any group medical insurance plan, take advantage of it. If not, compare the cost of Blue Cross/Blue Shield with other plans. Note the various features of each. Consider taking a larger deductible, so you'll have a smaller premium to pay.

VALERIE AND JAMES McQUARTER HAVE NO JOB BENEFITS...

...because they are self–employed. So they have had to shop carefully for insurance. They discovered that they could join a professional organization for musicians that provides group medical coverage for its members. This gives them enough coverage at a price they can afford—much lower than if they bought individual policies. Many professional groups and other associations, as well as trade unions, provide group insurance for their members.

Property and casualty insurance

What is the biggest investment you have? Probably your home—whether you own or rent. If you had a severe fire in your home, or a hurricane or flood roared through your town, or thieves broke in and took your TV and stereo and silver, could you make repairs and buy replacements out of your financial assets? Few of us could. That's why it's imperative that you cover your home with property and casualty insurance.

Most people understand the basic idea of this coverage: If a fire, theft, damage from wind or flood occur, we will be reimbursed for the loss. But few really understand what will be covered by the insurance company and what they must take care of themselves.

This kind of policy is called a "homeowner's" policy, but you don't have to be a homeowner to get it. Usually it covers:

1. Fire insurance on the house (i.e., the building itself).
2. Extended coverage for damage to the house (i.e., the building) by such things as wind, hail, falling objects, smoke, motor vehicles.
3. Allowance for additional living expenses if you have to live elsewhere while repairs are made.
4. Personal property lost because of fire, theft, other damage, or mysterious disappearance (this covers such items as clothing, books, cameras, stereos, all household furnishings).
5. Liability. This covers claims based on any injuries suffered by others on and caused by your property. Classic example: the mailman is bitten by your dog or slips on the ice on your sidewalk. The insurance coverage includes payments for medical expenses.

See Exhibit 7 for the six major types of homeowner policy, each identified by the name used by the insurance company.

Exhibit 7
GUIDE TO HOMEOWNERS POLICIES

These are the principal features of *standard* homeowners policies. Some will differ in a few respects from the standard ones. Policy conditions may also vary according to state requirements.

	HO-1 (basic form)	HO-2 (broad form)	HO-3 (special form)	HO-4 (renters' contents broad form)	HO-5 (comprehensive form)	HO-6 (for condominium owners)
PERILS COVERED (see key below)	perils 1–10	perils 1–17	perils 1–17 on personal property except glass breakage; all risks, except those specifically excluded, on buildings	perils 1–17	all risks except those specifically excluded	perils 1–17
STANDARD AMOUNT OF INSURANCE ON house and attached structures	based on property value, minimum $15,000	based on property value, minimum $15,000	based on property value, minimum $20,000	10% of personal insurance on additions and alterations to unit	based on property value, minimum $30,000	$1,000 on owner's additions and alterations to unit
detached structures	10% of amount of insurance on house	10% of amount of insurance on house	10% of amount of insurance on house	no coverage	10% of amount of insurance on house	no coverage
trees, shrubs, plants	5% of amount of insurance on house. $500 maximum per item	5% of amount of insurance on house. $500 maximum per item	5% of amount of insurance on house. $500 maximum per item	10% of personal property insurance, $500 maximum per item	5% of amount of insurance on house. $500 maximum per item	10% of personal property insurance, $500 maximum per item
personal property	50% of insurance on house; 10% for property normally kept at another residence, minimum $1,000	50% of insurance on house; 10% for property normally kept at another residence, minimum $1,000	50% of insurance on house; 10% for property normally kept at another residence, minimum $1,000	based on value of property, minimum $6,000; 10% for property normally kept at another residence, minimum $1,000	50% of insurance on house; 10% for property normally kept at another residence, minimum $1,000	based on value of property, minimum $6,000; 10% for property normally kept at another residence, minimum $1,000
loss of use, additional living expense; loss of rent if rental unit uninhabitable	10% of insurance on house	20% of insurance on house	20% of insurance on house	20% of personal property insurance	20% of insurance on house	40% of personal property insurance
SPECIAL LIMITS OF LIABILITY	Money, bank notes, bullion, gold other than goldware, silver other than silverware, platinum, coins, and medals—$100. Securities, accounts, deeds, manuscripts, passports, tickets, stamps, etc.—$500. Watercraft, including their trailers, furnishings, equipment, and outboard motors—$500. Trailers not used with watercraft—$500. Grave markers—$500. Theft of jewelry, watches, furs, precious and semiprecious stones—$500. Theft of silverware, silver-plated ware, goldware, gold-plated ware, and pewterware—$1,000. Theft of guns—$1,000.					
CREDIT CARD, FORGERY, COUNTERFEIT MONEY	$500	$500	$500	$500	$500	$500
COMPREHENSIVE PERSONAL LIABILITY	$25,000	$25,000	$25,000	$25,000	$25,000	$25,000
DAMAGE TO PROPERTY OF OTHERS	$250	$250	$250	$250	$250	$250
MEDICAL PAYMENTS	$500 per person	$500 per person	$500 per person	$500 per person	$500 per person	$500 per person

Key to perils covered
1. fire, lightning
2. windstorm, hail
3. explosion
4. riots
5. damage by aircraft
6. damage by vehicles not owned or operated by people covered by policy
7. damage from smoke
8. vandalism, malicious mischief
9. theft
10. glass breakage
11. falling objects
12. weight of ice, snow, sleet
13. collapse of building or any part of building
14. leakage or overflow of water or steam from a plumbing, heating or air-conditioning system
15. bursting, cracking, burning, or bulging of a steam or hot-water heating system, or of appliances for heating water
16. freezing of plumbing, heating, and air-conditioning systems and domestic appliances
17. injury to electrical appliances, devices, fixtures, and wiring (excluding tubes, transistors, and similar electronic components) from short circuits or other accidentally generated currents

Tips: Some things you should know about homeowner's insurance.

- The policy provides protection at a specified address, and usually *only* at that address. Most policies, however, will cover losses that occur when you are traveling or if possessions are in storage or, for instance, at the cleaner's. They won't cover losses suffered by a family member who is, in effect, living elsewhere—say, in a college dorm during the majority of the year. That's why my parents got so upset when I expected their insurance to cover my stolen stereo.

- Most policies limit the amount they will pay to the actual current cash value of the stolen or destroyed property. The insurance companies take the age of the article into account; they depreciate it for each year you have owned it. Since the actual cash value may be a lot lower than what you will have to pay to replace the item—especially the way property has appreciated in recent years—this practice by the insurance companies can be costly to you. You can, however, ask the insurance company to add a "replacement endorsement" (for payment at replacement value) to your policy for a modest increase in the premium. It will be worth having if a major loss occurs.

- As Exhibit 7 shows, the typical standard homeowner's policy limits the amount the company will pay for a loss of personal property. Usually, the limit is 50 percent of the total amount the building is insured for. The loss is also limited to fire, windstorm, and other specific perils (carefully listed in the policy). If you have some special things that are valuable—antique furniture, an art collection, jewelry, silver, or books—ask for a "personal property floater schedule." This will give you extra coverage. It can be expensive, however. The insurance company will want to have appraisals made, giving a cash value to everything you put on the schedule. If you take out this kind of coverage, be sure to reevaluate these items at least every couple of years, as their value will rise with inflation and may change depending on the market for them. Also, update the list regularly to delete any items you no longer possess, and add any new ones. Usually, to help keep the premium cost down, this kind of coverage has a deductible amount. *Note:* If you are carrying a personal property floater on your homeowner's policy, your own record keeping—including an inventory of items, receipts for purchases, and photographs of items—will be vital.

Homeowners are not the only ones who need coverage. If you are renting, you need personal property and liability coverage just as much as if you are the owner. A person who slips on your rented sidewalk, for instance, can sue you as well as the landlord. So talk to an insurance agent or broker about a tenant's policy. It could provide repayment for theft of your newly acquired wedding gifts or your spanking new appliances or other purchases. It could pay for smoke damage from a fire in the apartment next door to you.

If you're a condominium owner, ask about a special insurance form. You're really kind of halfway between being a tenant and a homeowner. Make sure the condo association is carrying insurance on the common elements: the building itself and the recreational areas, hallways, driveways, and parking spaces you share with your neighbors. But make sure you are covered, as owners of your condo, for everything within your own unit: the interior walls, bathroom and kitchen fixtures, appliances and cabinets, all your household goods, and personal property. And don't forget liability insurance. The association must, of course, carry liability, but if someone should be seriously injured, for instance, in the commonly owned pool, each of you who are unit owners could be assessed to cover any damages above and beyond the association's insurance. The insurance people call this a Loss Assessment Endorsement. You may have to ask specifically for it to be added to your policy, so check the association's policy and have your broker or agent make sure your own policy picks up where the association's leaves off.

How much insurance should you carry on your home? It depends on the replacement value of what you're insuring—the building and its contents. What's important, again, is regular review. You cannot just let your homeowner's policy sit there while you renew it year after year, because inflation as well as the general appreciation of real estate are both adding up all the time to greater replacement cost. Most insurance companies and their agents add an increment every year for that upward spiral, and simply bill you for the increase.

Ask yourselves these questions:

- Are we buying collectibles that call for special insurance?
- Should we get appraisals of certain valuables—antiques, heirlooms—so we can take out a personal property floater?
- Since the floater is relatively expensive, do we want to insure only those items that would be really difficult to replace, such as heirlooms?
- Are we keeping smaller items in a safe–deposit box at the bank—a less expensive way to handle the risk?

Put up an umbrella, too

An "umbrella liability policy" could be valuable insurance on a rainy day. It provides coverage that your homeowner's or your automobile insurance policies do not provide: coverage of special situations. Say your dog inflicts really terrible damage on the mailman—more than your homeowner's liability covers—or you knock over a pile of antique china in a china shop and are sued for damages. (For this, for example, homeowner's will pay you a maximum of $500 despite the fact that you managed to destroy $1,200 worth of china). An umbrella policy can cover the difference. Cost? For an annual premium of about $100, you can get about $1 million in coverage.

Lawsuits are no fun

You should be aware that while liability insurance protects you against lawsuits by the person bitten by your dog or injured on your icy sidewalk, it does *not* cover you in a situation where a repairperson, housekeeper, gardener, or painter is injured while working in your home. They should be covered by worker's compensation. Never assume that a repair-person or housepainter or other contractor has his or her own insurance. Ask to see proof.

How much liability insurance is enough? The range carried by most people runs from $25,000 to $300,000. Knowing how many liability claims there are these days and the size of some of the settlements you read about in the papers, you can well imagine that coverage for as much as $1 million is not a bad idea if you have a fairly substantial combined income and assets. Lawyers who are suing for injured parties usually try for as much as they can, and they dig the well where the water is.

Automobile Insurance

In most states the law requires auto insurance. If you live where it is not required, and if you drive without it, you are asking for trouble. A single accident could put you into financial disaster.

You should be informed on five aspects of auto insurance:

1. *Liability coverage.* This protects you, the owner of the car, from claims that may result from the injury or death of another person or from damage to property. The other person may be a pedestrian or passenger or driver of another vehicle. The situation itself may be almost anything; the newspapers regularly report crazy vehicular accidents that no one could have anticipated. The property? It could be another vehicle or a tree, fence, building, or any other stationary object.

   When you look at an automobile insurance policy, you see figures like this: $100,000/$300,000-$25,000. What do they mean? The first two figures indicate that the insurance company will pay up to $100,000 for bodily injuries to any one person, and up to $300,000 for injuries to two more persons in any one accident. The $25,000 means they will pay that maximum for property damage.

2. *Collision.* This pays for damage to your car caused by a collision with some other vehicle or with any other object, whether stationary or moving. Usually, to cut down on the premium cost, it carries a deductible of $100 to $300, so you will pay for minor repairs yourself. This saves the insurance company from having to

handle small claims for minor damage, which would greatly increase their overhead costs and thus raise everyone's costs. Usually the insurance company pays for the cost of all repairs higher than the deductible. If the car is totaled, the company pays the actual cash value of the car, less your deductible amount. How much collision coverage you get thus depends on the type, make, and age of the car. The company is never obligated to pay more for repairs than the car was worth before the accident, less the salvage value of the car. Most insurance companies will let you choose how much deductible you want to risk; the higher your risk, the lower your premium cost.

3. *Comprehensive.* Many factors, in addition to driving accidents caused by you or by someone else, are capable of damaging your car: fire, theft, wind, hail, falling objects, to name a few. So you need comprehensive insurance to cover them. Again, a deductibility clause may reduce your premium.

4. *Medical payments.* This section of your policy covers any passengers who may be injured while riding in your car. It usually also covers any members of your family who are injured while riding in any other vehicle.

5. *No–fault insurance.* The basic principle of liability insurance is that one person must be to blame for an accident in order for another person to qualify for compensation. But proving whose fault it was is not always possible, and it nearly always takes time and may involve a lawsuit. As a result, in order to eliminate the need for liability suits, many states have adopted no–fault insurance laws. Their objective is to make your insurance company pay for your losses, while the other person's pays for his or hers. Under no–fault law, unless the expenses covered by no–fault exceed a certain dollar limit, you may not take action against the other party.

What is the basis for insurance rates? It's a highly complex procedure. Each insurance company periodically computes its income from premiums in each state in which it is entitled to write insurance. Obviously, no company is in business to lose money;

each must take in enough to cover what it pays out to settle claims as well as cover its overhead costs and maintain a profit margin. The total amount of premiums in the state is divided among various territories within the state. In each such area, the company establishes a set of base premiums for the individual coverages (liability, collision, comprehensive, medical) that make up an auto insurance policy. These base rates are considered to pertain to a stereotype: an adult male (usually over the age of 25) driving a standard car only for pleasure, not business. Using that as a base, everyone who buys a policy pays more or less than a standard rate, depending on how the company sees him or her as a risk in relation to this stereotypical person.

In effect, you are assigned to a group according to characteristics that the company (or "underwriters") believe predict the group's chances of creating insurance losses. Out of this comes the typical situation in which a policyholder in a large urban area pays more for "the same insurance" than one in a small town or suburban area.

What are some of those characteristics or criteria that determine where you land on the scale? Age, sex, and marital status; record of accidents and previous traffic violations; type of car, number of cars in the family, and mileage traveled in a year; use of the car for pleasure, business, daily commutation, or farming. Each such characteristic is assigned a numerical weight based on its tendency to increase or decrease the probability of an insurance claim or loss. The possible combinations of such rating factors is just about limitless, and it seems to get more complicated every year.

The extreme example of how the total numerical weight of various characteristics could affect *you* is the experience some of you had when you started to drive as an unmarried male under the age of 25. Your parents' auto insurance premium probably doubled—a fact that hit home if they insisted that you pay for the difference. And you have no doubt been aware of this ever since. Now, if you are over 25, or married, or both, you are seeing a decrease in those horrendous premium costs. (Good reminder: If you haven't notified the insurance company of a change in marital status, do so; it could save you some money.)

Tips: If you have an accident, and you've never had one before, remember:

- Your agent should be your best ally. When you are buying auto insurance, find an agent or broker who will assist you in every way and work on your behalf. The policy may not be the lowest–cost one, but the service he or she provides in the event of an accident will be worth its weight in gold.
- When you are filing a claim, you cannot avoid running around to get the estimates the insurance company requires. Certain things must be done, and they take time.
- Always keep your cool in car insurance matters. Do not get rattled. If the insurance company sends an adjuster to estimate damage, don't let this person get to you. Stay calm. Be firm. And try not to talk too much. If you feel you are not satisfied, ask to speak to the adjuster's superior.

When you are buying auto insurance or reviewing what you have, keep these points in mind:

1. Nothing stays the same. Policies must be reviewed and updated regularly.
2. Premium rates vary according to where you live and according to the amount of risk you are willing to shoulder yourself by accepting higher deductibility.
3. Liability coverage should be the absolute maximum you can get. If you have substantial assets, you need substantial liability coverage. Anyone who decides to sue you will go for all they can get.
4. Your car's value diminishes as it gets older. Keep an eye on its cash value. If you own the car long enough, the annual premiums for collision coverage will begin to approach the replacement value of the car. When that happens, it's time to stop buying collision coverage.
5. Shop around for auto insurance. It is high–priced stuff, and many companies are competing for your business. Best approach: Work with an independent broker who will get you the best coverage for the lowest premium cost. Talk to several brokers before you decide.

Some insurance you may never need

Flight insurance is sold at airport counters and through automatic machines. Do you need it? Remember that fewer people die in air crashes than in car accidents, poisonings, accidental falls, or from choking on food. If you buy your airline tickets on some charge cards, they automatically cover you with life insurance during your flight.

When you rent a car, you are usually asked if you want coverage—for an additional fee—in case the rental car gets into an accident. This usually covers the deductible, for which the rental company would hold you responsible. Check your own policy—it may cover you while driving a rented car.

Heard about pet insurance? It's been offered since 1982. One such policy costs from $50 to $80 for up to $2,000 coverage. When "Baby" cashed in one of his nine lives by falling out a fourth-floor window, an operation to save the other eight lives left both front paws in casts—plenty expensive. Next, he was rushed 120 miles round–trip every day for weeks to get special radiation treatments. Pet insurance would have been mighty nice to have.

Summary

Whatever insurance you are considering and reviewing—life, health, disability, property and casualty, or automobile—you should ask yourselves some basic questions:

What if? What if this, what if that? What risks do we take? What things could possibly happen?

Which of these risks must we assume ourselves, and which can we pay an insurance company to take over? That, in turn, will determine what kinds of policies and coverage are needed.

How much will it cost? Shop around. Get several quotes, or bids, from various agents and companies. Make your decisions based on coverage, service, and cost.

Are we carrying enough insurance—or too much—for our situation right now? Updating and reevaluating policies every so often is most important.

Worksheet X: Yours
HOW MUCH LIFE INSURANCE?

A. ANNUAL FAMILY LIVING COSTS (from Budget form) _____

B. SOURCES OF INCOME AVAILABLE

●Spouse's Income _____

●Social Security Benefits _____

●Income from Income-Producing
Assets (from Budget form) _____

●Income from Proceeds of Existing Life Insurance Policies
(use an assumed rate of interest)

  6%—multiply amount of insurance by .06
10%—multiply amount of insurance by .10
12%—multiply amount of insurance by .12

_____ × .10 = _____

●Other Sources of Income _____

TOTAL SOURCES OF INCOME _____

C. ADDITIONAL INCOME NEEDED (subtract B from A) _____

D. AMOUNT OF MONEY TO MAKE UP SHORTAGE
(at an assumed rate of interest)

  6%—divide by .06
10%—divide by .10
12%—divide by .12

_____ ÷ .10 _____

E. ADDITIONAL CASH REQUIREMENTS

Final Expenses _____

Education for Children _____

Liabilities (including Mortgage) _____ _____

F. INSURANCE NEEDS (D plus E) _____

Worksheet XI: Yours
HOW MUCH DISABILITY INSURANCE?

A. ANNUAL FAMILY EXPENSES   _____

B. SOURCES OF INCOME

    • Spouse's Net Income _____

    • Social Security Benefits _____

    • Disability Benefits from Work _____

    Income from Income-Producing Assets
    (Assets Evaluation form) _____

    • Other Income_____

    TOTAL SOURCES OF INCOME   _____

C. ADDITIONAL ANNUAL INCOME NEEDED
(Subtract B from A)   _____

D. MONTHLY BENEFIT NEEDED   _____

SAVING AND INVESTING FOR NOW AND THE FUTURE

12

The difference between saving and investing

There are important differences. Saving is accumulating money for a specific purpose or to use in an emergency. It is a way of preserving capital and guaranteeing steady income. It is also a way of maintaining liquidity. You can always get at your money if it is put away in savings.

Investing is different. You take a chance when you invest. You accept risk—on the premise that you will get better returns.

Investing not only involves risk. It involves your time and effort. You must be willing to devote time to it, to study, listen, compare, and make sometimes difficult choices. Investing is a much more active exercise than saving.

Saving is passive. Investing is active.

If you are looking for growth for your money, it is time to begin an investment program. The important thing to remember is that investing takes time—and don't try to outguess the market. Over the long haul there will be slumps, but there will be those unexpected rallies. Saving

is itself one of the foundation stones for investing. For you must have a solid foundation upon which to build an investment program. Such a foundation consists of several fundamentals, including:

* savings for an emergency
* savings for one or more specific goals
* adequate life insurance
* IRA or 401(k)
* a home of your own

And you need one more fundamental: enough income to use for investing. Only when you have enough income to meet living and saving expenses and maintain a positive cash flow, or liquidity, should you consider yourselves ready to take the risks that are involved in investing in stocks and bonds or any of the other possibilities of "the market."

Savings accounts

Money in a checking account is like cash in your pocket. It burns a hole. It will be spent.

Having at least one savings account is a must. Open one when you open your checking account or accounts. And start the habit of paying yourself immediately after payday by putting money into your reserve for emergency fund and fixed expenses.

1. *Passbook savings.* This is the old standby. Its chief advantage is that your money is available any time you want it, without your paying any penalty for taking it out. Its disadvantage is that it doesn't pay as much interest as other types of accounts. Not all passbook accounts are alike, so:

   • Shop around to see where you can get the best deal on interest.
   • Watch out for evaporation: Some banks impose a $5 service charge every month on accounts with less than a $300 balance (if you have $100 in a passbook account in such a bank and you forget it for a year, you will have $40 in the account).
   • Ask how interest is credited: Is it compounded annually, semiannually, quarterly, or daily? The answer tells you where you will get the highest *effective yield*, or total interest paid on the account. (How do you figure out *compound interest?* To your balance, or principal amount, you add the interest earned for the period—year, half-year, month, or day—to get a new principal amount. Then calculate the interest on *that*, and add it, for still another new principal. Obviously, the more frequently the interest is compounded, the higher the effective yield. What you want, ideally, is interest compounded daily from day of deposit to day of withdrawal.)
   • Check also on *when* interest is credited. In some banks, even though compounding is daily, the money earned may not be credited to your account until the end of a three–month period. If you withdraw money before it is credited, you can lose the interest on it for the entire three–month period. Again, day–of–deposit to day–of–withdrawal compounding is what you want.

2. *Money market account.* While not as tightly regulated as they were a few years ago, these accounts, which pay higher interest than passbook savings, usually start with a minimum deposit of $1,000.

   • You have instant access to the account and you incur no penalties.
   • Banks may determine their own rates of interest, based on what they consider to be market conditions, so careful shopping around is called for.
   • Banks may not *guarantee* a rate of interest for longer than one month. Most guarantee by the week; this keeps them competitive with the popular money market funds on Wall Street.
   • The chief advantage is that you can have your money market account in the same bank as your checking account and transfer funds when you need them, thus earning interest until you need to use the cash.

3. *CDs or TDs.* Certificates of deposit or time deposits are also worth considering. With these, you are committed to keeping a certain amount of money on deposit for a minimum period. These fixed–term savings were deregulated on Oct. 1, 1983. Every bank may now set its own minimum investment size and interest rate; and while there used to be specific time limits, you may now purchase a certificate for virtually any term you want—from three months to 10 years. You may also decide on the maturity date you want. Want a certificate to mature on your wedding anniversary or on a child's birthday? Just say so when you're buying it. You may select the term or the interest rate and the bank will design a certificate to match what you want.

   Deregulated investments demand close scrutiny. Take the time to read the bank advertisements and ask hard questions. The choices are many, and so are the decisions you will have to make.

   Tip: With deregulation, the penalties that used to be imposed if you withdrew your money before the maturity date have been relaxed. They are far less severe.

"The market" and its risks

The typical investor faces a bewildering range of choices: stocks, bonds, mutual funds, real estate,

Exhibit 8
COMPOUND INTEREST CHART
End-of-Year Values

Investing small amounts of money over time can prove to be very profitable. The chart below shows the effect of $1,200 per year ($100 per month) invested at varying rates compounded *annually*.

End-of-Year Values	6%	8%	10%
5th year	$7,170	$7,603	$8,059
10th year	16,766	18,774	21,037
20th year	46,791	59,307	75,602
30th year	100,562	146,815	217,131
40th year	196,857	335,737	584,222

tangible goods, precious metals and a good many other alternatives.

Besides all the choices, there is no shortage of people to give you advice: brokers, analysts, accountants, lawyers, etc. Remember, it is your money, and you may want to participate in the decisions to buy or to hold certain investments. Not only should you understand your investments, but the most important key is to be comfortable with the way that your money is invested. You hear stories about people who have "made a killing in the market." You dream that one of those people could be you. But what you seldom hear is that for every one who has made a killing there is a loser—someone who took the risk that goes with investing and then took a loss. That's why it is vital that you establish the solid financial foundation you need.

The loser who was prepared to lose and took the risk is in one situation. Unhappy, yes, but not in trouble. But the loser who could not afford to lose is in trouble. There are few sadder moments than when you find you need the money you have invested for some other purpose, decide to sell, and discover that you must sell at a loss and get back less than you had before.

So you must understand that investing is risky, and you must figure out what your "risk temperature" is—no two people ever have exactly the same one.

One person may feel comfortable investing in blue–chip stocks while another keeps her cool best in tax–sheltered limited partnerships, and a third goes in for municipal bonds. No one should ever be talked into any type of investment that makes him or her feel uncomfortable. Yet you cannot make money without taking some risks, and the faster you hope to make it—and the greater the amount you hope to make—the greater the risks you will have to take. What kind of risks? Here are some to consider, but note that you, as an investor, have little control over them.

- *Macroeconomic risk.* Change in monetary policy. Outbreak of war. Change in OPEC policy.
- *Market risk.* Shifts in capital flows and psychology, unrelated to economic news, that can cause advances or declines in the market (e.g., changes in interest rates).
- *Industry risk.* Changing circumstances within a particular industry: for example, the changes in the automotive industry brought about by OPEC and by fuel–efficient imports.
- *Business risk.* The competitor of the company whose stock you buy comes out with a better product than your company's.
- *Management risk.* Mergers, reorganizations, results of poor management judgment—even an unforeseen event (a plane crash, a fire).
- *Information risk.* Rumors or information that are misleading or false.
- *Natural disaster risk.* Floods, hurricanes, drought, tornadoes that could affect, for example, a livestock or crop investment.
- *Liquidity risk.* Insufficient demand for your investment when you decide to sell (or when you *must* sell to gain cash).

Decide on investment objectives

How do you decide what your investment goals are? Ask yourselves these questions:

1. Are we looking for income and high yield: steady income that we can depend on, at a fairly high percentage of the investment?
2. Are we looking for current growth: Do we want to see our investment itself grow steadily—and not be so concerned about its producing

income—so it will be worth a lot more when we sell it?

3. Are we looking for *aggressive* growth—do we want to make some quick bucks, then sell and do it again?

4. Are we investing to gain tax advantages (e.g., maybe defer taxes or buy tax–free municipal bonds)?

The answer to questions such as these can help you set some investment objectives. You should plan your strategy before you buy specific investments. The issue isn't where the market is but what your needs are. Your goals will also be determined by your ages, your temperaments, your current and future financial needs.

Once you have set your objectives—and it is a good idea to write them down and file them with your investment papers—you must stick to them until the time comes when you know they should be changed. If your income is moving upward and you do not have children to feed, clothe, and educate, your needs probably run in the direction of investing for growth and for tax advantages. If your children are in the expensive teenage and college years, or you're retired, you'll be looking for income and high yield.

What type of investment?

Assuming that you have looked carefully at your budget and net worth and have decided you have enough income to maintain a positive cash flow and take care of expenses, let's look at the kinds of investing you'll want to consider.

1. *Government securities.* Since the U.S. government borrows $200 billion a year, new issues are readily available. These are safe investments simply because the government can print new dollars to repay old debts. There are three types of government securities:

   • Treasury bills. Sold every week, these reach maturity within three, six, or 12 months. The minimum investment is $10,000. You buy them at a discount. For example, if you buy a three–month Treasury bill worth $10,000, it is possible to be purchased for $9,850. Three months later it could be presented for full payment of $10,000, realizing $150 in interest.

   • Treasury notes. These are sold every four weeks or so. They mature in anywhere from one to 10 years and usually require a minimum investment of $5,000. You pay the full value of the note you buy, and you get cash interest from the government twice a year during the term of the note.

   • Treasury bonds. These are not sold on a regular schedule. You have to watch for them (check with your banker regularly if you are interested). Treasury bonds take anywhere from 10 to 30 years to mature, so they are definitely in the long–range category. Usually you can get them for $1,000 apiece. Like treasury notes, they pay cash interest twice a year and you buy them at full face value.

Where do you buy Treasuries? You can purchase them directly at any Federal Reserve Bank. You can buy them through the mail, but this requires a certified check one week in advance. You can also buy them through a broker or a bank (either will add a sales charge).

Tip: If you buy Treasuries through the mail, you won't know what interest rate you are getting until after you have made the purchase.

Hold on to Treasuries until they mature. You can always borrow against them or sell them in the secondary market, where you will get more or less what you paid for them, depending on whether the interest rates have fallen, risen, or stayed the same since you bought them.

Note: Treasuries are not taxed at the state or local level. If you live in a state that imposes a tax on interest income, Treasuries can thus give you a certain tax advantage.

2. *Government savings bonds.* The government now pays a floating interest rate on savings bonds. The rate will increase if interest rates go up and, if held for five years, the bonds will pay

a guaranteed minimum return. The interest is exempt from state and local taxes and no Federal tax is due until the bonds mature or are cashed in. Series HH bonds may be purchased only in exchange for EE bonds, with interest also deferred until maturity. Savings bonds have excellent liquidity—you may cash them in after holding six months at any bank—and they are extremely safe, but their yields are lower than other investments that are just as safe. Why buy them? One reason is that you can't afford any larger kind of government security. Another reason is to force yourselves to save, by buying them through a payroll deduction plan. *Note:* like other treasuries, savings bonds are not taxed at the state or local level.

3. *Corporate bonds.* When you buy a bond, whether it is a government bond or a corporate bond, you are lending your money to that particular government body or corporation for a specified length of time. At the end of that time, that is, the date of maturity, the issuer of the bond pays you back the full amount, or face value, of the bond. Meanwhile, you receive a fixed rate of interest, paid twice a year in most cases. The rate of interest is imprinted on the bond. A 9 percent rate means that a $1,000 bond will pay you $90 a year. This rate does not change once the bond is issued, whether or not bond prices fluctuate.

What is the risk in bonds? The credit worthiness of the corporation that issued the bond can deteriorate. And, as interest rates rise, the value of the bond drops. Bonds that were issued a number of years ago are likely to have lost their value because interest rates are so much higher than they were when the bonds were issued. Such bonds are called *discount bonds*.

Here's an example of how they work:

Bond prices move up and down with changes in interest rates because yields on existing bonds must compete with those on new bonds that are being issued. Let's say that interest rates go up after you have purchased a $1,000 bond with a 9 percent rate. If interest rates rise to 10 percent, no one will pay $1,000 for your 9 percent bond. The price of the bond will drop to roughly $900,

so that its yield to maturity will be 10 percent. The yield to maturity takes into account the coupon rate of 9 percent and any gain or loss in the price of the bond between the time when you buy it and the maturity date. When purchasing a bond after it has been issued, make sure you ask the broker what the yield to maturity is. Bond prices are also dependent on the length of time between purchase and maturity. The longer the term to maturity, the more volatile the price. The price of a 10 percent coupon bond with a 30-year maturity will generally fall about 8.7 percent if interest rates rise one percentage point. But a 10 percent bond due in three years will drop about 2.5 percent with a similar rise in rates. So a change in interest rates affects the price of a bond with a longer time to mature than one with shorter maturity. Buy CD's, bonds and Treasuries with varying maturities. That way you reinvest more often, taking advantage of increases in interest rates that might have occurred. And if interest rates fall, some of your savings will be locked in at higher rates.

The opposite of all this is that if interest rates go down, a bond increases in value and can be sold at a premium.

In a word, bonds adjust—they adjust to interest movements by changing price.

4. *Tax–exempt bonds.* States, communities and their agencies issue bonds that are usually called "municipals." Their yields are not taxed by the federal government. These are usually recommended only for people in high income brackets. In deciding between tax-free and taxable bonds, you have to figure the tax–equivalent yield—i.e., the yield a taxable bond would need to equal that of a tax–exempt issue. The answer depends on your Federal and state income tax rates. If you are in the 28 percent tax bracket and live in Connecticut, a tax–exempt yield of 6 percent would be equivalent to a 9.46 percent taxable bond. Bonds with longer maturities will provide extra yield. *Tip:* You avoid not only the federal tax but any state or local taxes when you buy a bond issued by the state you live in.

5. *Mortgage–backed securities*, such as those issued by the Government National Mortgage

Association (GNMA), are pools of mortgage loans. The government guarantees the payment of interest and principal but it does not guarantee that market value won't fluctuate. Interest and a small amount of principal are paid to you each month. If interest rates drop, borrowers might either sell or refinance their homes. As a result you might receive a return of a lot of your principal, which you will be investing at lower interest rates. The actual yield of a mortgage security depends on the extent to which the underlying loans are paid off ahead of time. The yields on GNMA's are usually higher than on long–term treasuries. GNMA certificates come in $25,000 lots, but many investors invest in managed funds for an investment of $1,000 or more.

6. *Zero–coupon bonds* are sold at a deep discount from face value and pay interest at maturity. These are good for such long–term investment as retirement or for education of a child. The longer the maturity, the higher the rate of interest. You can purchase zero–coupon Treasuries, corporate or municipal bonds, but note that zeros pay no current interest. Unless you purchase tax–free or municipal zeros you must pay income tax on the deferred or "phantom income." The value of a zero will fluctuate with interest rates, but there is no effect if you hold it to maturity. One nice advantage: You can purchase varying maturity dates to coincide with such particular needs as tuition payments.

7. *The stock market.*   A stock market investment means that you become a part owner of a corporation. You buy a share in it. There are two obvious reasons for making such an investment.

  • You believe the company will succeed and that the price of its stock will rise as a result, and eventually you can sell your share in it for more than you paid for it.
  • You believe that while you own a share in it, the company will be so well run that it will make a profit and that the company will divide that profit among its shareholders, including you.

In the stock market, you will find no guarantees. A company may do well, or it may not. Stock prices change daily and if you are the nervous type who could be easily upset by a slight drop in the market price of a stock you own, you probably should not be in the market. You must also be willing to do your homework. You should never buy a stock that you have not studied thoroughly, so you know what kind of company issued it, who runs the company, what its goals are, what its record is. Such study is, of course, the specialty of the *securities analyst*, who works full time at this.

Your best approach to the market is through a good stockbroker. Shop for one as you shopped for your banker. Find a person who will take the time and make the effort to understand you and your particular needs. If a stockbroker fails to ask about your entire financial situation—your savings program, your insurance coverage, your respective incomes, your net worth today—he or she is not worth *your* time or your commission payments. If you really know what you're doing, and can choose your own stocks or bonds without assistance, consider using a discount broker, whose commissions for executing a trade are anywhere from 40 to 70 percent less than those of a regular broker.

Stocks are bought and sold, or traded, on exchanges. The largest in the United States is the New York Stock Exchange. That's where the major stocks—shares in the blue–chip corporations—are traded. The American Stock Exchange (AMEX) generally lists stocks of smaller, less well known companies. In addition there are regional exchanges located in other major cities. Many stocks are "unlisted" or sold "over–the–counter."

Tip: To get an idea of the listings, open the business section of a good daily newspaper and you will find them. *The New York Times* or *The Wall Street Journal* will give you the most comprehensive listings.

To buy or sell stocks, you must go through a stockbroker or any bank. The broker or the bank charges a commission on each transaction— buying or selling. The commission rate will vary, depending on whether it is a full–service or a discount brokerage service.

The risk in the market? That depends. On the economy in general. On the stock you buy. You can lose your shirt. You can make a bundle.

Tip: These are tips on what to do if you're going into investing in the stock market; "tips," or advice based on rumors, in the market are something else, and usually they are worthless:

- If you are looking for income, look for stocks that pay regular dividends.
- If you are looking for growth over a long period, buy stock in companies that show clear signs of growing. Probably they will not be paying out high dividends right now, but instead investing their profits in research and expansion to make the company grow.
- If you are building a portfolio of stocks for the long term, do *not* put all your eggs in one basket. Diversification is a must. Buy stocks of companies in several industries, and make different types of investments.

What about mutual funds?

If you are new to investing and can't decide where to begin, consider a mutual fund. The mutual fund gives you a way to spread out your risk and, in effect, buy diversification in a single purchase. With an investment of $1,000 in some mutual funds, you become part owner of a variety of stocks. The fund is managed by professionals who devote their full time to studying the market and making investment decisions. Because you are pooling your investment with thousands of others, the mutual fund gives you an ideal way to invest on a moderate scale.

A fund receives interest and dividend income and realizes gains and losses on its investments, then distributes its profits to you in proportion to the number of shares in the fund that you own. Funds make distributions at various times—some monthly, others quarterly, semiannually or annually.

You will find a wide variety of mutual funds available. They have various investment goals, which they address by concentrating on different types of securities. Selecting the fund category that suits you best requires balancing your tolerance for risk against the investment's expected return. Once you have decided on a mutual fund, you will be relieved of the need to study specific stocks and make decisions on them. The professional managers of the fund do that.

The various types of mutual funds are:

- *Income fund.* Designed to return a high level of income, these funds are invested in bonds, preferred stocks, and high–yielding common stocks.
- *Growth fund.* If you are looking for long–range capital gains, keep in mind these funds that are invested in companies that are expected to grow faster than the rate of inflation. Emphasis is on preserving capital, but with an effort to produce dividends.
- *Maximum capital gains fund.* The idea here is to go for big profits, usually by investing in small companies and in developing industries. These funds concentrate on more volatile issues and, as you might expect, the greater the push for high profits, the greater the risk.
- *Specialized fund.* In this category, you might find a fund that buys stocks of many companies in a single field, such as high tech. Usually, specialized funds concentrate on only one or two industries.
- *Tax–free fund.* These are invested in municipal bonds. They appeal to those who are in a high income bracket where tax–free income is desirable.
- *Balanced fund.* The balance is between stocks and bonds, with the idea of providing both income and capital appreciation.
- *Money market fund.* These large funds (many are gigantic) buy a wide variety of interest–yielding securities, including short–term certificates of deposit in large denominations, U.S. Treasury bills, and other short–term assets.

Cost of mutual fund investing

Mutual funds are either "load" or "no–load." A load fund is bought through a broker, who charges a commission (the load is the commission, or sales charge). If you buy directly from a specific fund, there is no sales charge; it is no–load.

Exhibit 9
MUTUAL FUND
RECORD OF TRANSACTIONS

Confirm Date	Trade Date	Transaction		Dollar Amount	Share Price	Shares This Transaction	Share Balance
10/3	10/3	Purchase		1,000.00	19.97	50,058	50.058
01/06	12/23	INCOME REINVEST	.550	27.53	22.15	1.243	51.301
01/06	12/23	SHORT TERM C G	.430	21.52	22.15	0.972	52.273
01/06	12/23	CAP GAIN REINV	1.670	83.60	22.15	3.774	56.047
03/28	03/14	INCOME REINVEST	.300	16.81	24.16	0.696	56.743
04/15	04/15	PURCHASE		695.00	24.37	28.519	85.262
06/28	06/14	INCOME REINVEST	.300	25.58	25.17	1.016	86.278
09/27	09/13	INCOME REINVEST	.300	25.88	24.98	1.036	87.314
Cost basis 9/27							1,895.92

A redemption fee may be charged when you sell shares in a mutual fund. Some redemption fees are imposed to discourage frequent trading. The fee may be set at very high levels for short holding periods. For instance, a fund may charge a 5 percent redemption fee on the sale of shares sold within one year of purchase, while shares sold in the second year incur a 4 percent fee, and so on down to 1 percent in the fifth year, then nothing thereafter. Others impose small redemption fees at all times.

Nearly all funds allow the interest and capital gains to be reinvested without a sales charge. However, a few funds impose "reloading" charges on the reinvestment of capital gains distributions. There is a growing tendency for some funds to have a "hidden" load charge. These funds—known as "12b-1" plans—may charge up to 1.25 percent per year. The money may be used only to advertise and promote the fund to prospective investors. In addition to loads, reloading and hidden loads, all funds require their shareholders to share the operating expenses, transaction costs and portfolio fees that a fund incurs each year. These fees usually range from .25 percent to 1 percent per year.

The success of your mutual fund depends, of course, on market conditions, but the idea of the fund is to spread the risk of owning securities. The return you get depends on the type of fund you decide to get into. An income fund will emphasize dividends, while a growth fund will give you smaller dividends but greater capital gains.

Taxing of mutual funds

Income distributions from mutual funds are taxed as ordinary income, whether you receive a check during the year or have the distributions reinvested. Each fund you own will send you a 1099-DIV. For each mutual fund you are in, keep accurate records to determine what you paid for the original shares and all the reinvested shares. This will help you calculate your profits when you sell the shares. You want to avoid double taxation on the reinvested distributions—investors need to add the amount of reinvested distributions to their original purchase price when determining a capital gain or loss. Many investors in mutual funds fail to keep accurate records as they reinvest. Thus they pay taxes twice on their reinvested distributions. For example: Suppose you buy $1,000 of shares in a mutual fund and receive $200 of distributions on which you pay taxes—and then you sell the shares for $1,500. The taxable profit is based on the original cost of the shares—$1,000—

plus the $200 of taxed distribution. Thus, the taxable gain would be $300, instead of $500.

When you sell shares in a mutual fund, it is a taxable event. If you redeem or sell all your shares, there is no problem about having to sort out how many shares you have been sold. Many people will sell only part of their shares without specifying what shares they want sold. It is then assumed that the first in are the first sold (FIFO) or, those you owned the longest are sold first. You can, however, specify what shares you want sold. Your gain or loss is then based on what those particular shares cost when you bought them. You must keep careful records and advise the fund about exactly which shares you want sold.

A mutual fund's total net assets (the total of all the stocks and bonds and other investments it has bought) are divided by the number of shares it has outstanding (i.e., all the shares that have been bought by people who have invested in the mutual fund). This gives the value of one share in the fund—called the *net asset value*. The net asset value rises and falls with the market prices of the fund's holdings. It is figured daily. The number of shares you buy when you invest depends on the amount you are investing divided by the net asset value on the day you make your purchase. For example, in a no–load fund, if you invest $1,000 on a day when the net asset value is $21.21, you will own 47.147 shares of that particular fund.

If you are the type of person who has real self–discipline, you might go for dollar–cost averaging—a conservative approach to investing in mutual funds. What you do is invest a fixed sum of money at regular intervals, regardless of the market. The idea is that you lower your average cost per share by buying more shares when the prices are low and fewer when the prices are high. Dollar–cost averaging is a long–term strategy. What you must do is ignore all fluctuations in the market and stick to your plan. That's where the self–discipline comes in: Maintain your dollar–cost averaging no matter what happens from day to day, not allowing the market or your emotions to change your strategy.

Investing in mutual funds is one of the easiest and most convenient ways to begin your investment program. Most funds can be opened with $1,000. Some are lower. Others are higher. Important tip: If you are planning to use dollar–cost averaging, make sure the minimum amount required by the fund after the initial investment is not higher than the amount you had planned to invest.

Before you invest in a mutual fund, look over your needs and objectives carefully—and study up on mutual funds. You will find annual surveys on the performance of mutual funds in many magazines. Compare their performance, noting especially how they do when the market is good and when it is bad.

Mutual funds give you a number of advantages:

1. *Small minimum investment.*   A small amount can get you started, and subsequent purchases can be even smaller.
2. *Diversification.*   Each share you buy in a mutual fund gives you an interest in a broad range of stocks, bonds, or any other kind of investment the fund specializes in. Diversification helps soften the blow that can come from wide price fluctuations when you own individual securities. Diversification limits risk.
3. *Liquidity.*   When you want to sell, the mutual fund will always buy back its shares—at a time, you hope, when you will realize a gain and not a loss.
4. *Automatic reinvestment.*   You can ask most funds to reinvest, automatically, dividends earned, so your account keeps growing. Capital gains can be reinvested, too.
5. *Automatic withdrawal.*   If you want regular cash income as your fund produces dividends, most will set up an automatic withdrawal plan for you. (This can be particularly valuable in your retirement years—far from now.)
6. *Exchange privilege.*   Since many funds manage a "family" of different kinds of mutual funds, they can let you switch your investment from one type to another as your needs and objectives change or as you want to take advantage of changes in the market, known as "investment timing." But it is important to remember that when you switch, you are selling shares in one fund and buying shares in another. If there is a gain on the fund, you will have to pay taxes on that gain.

Annuities

An annuity is an investment contract. It is purchased from an insurance company. The idea is to provide the annuitant (the person who buys the annuity) with payments at regular intervals over a fixed period, starting some time in the future. The money in an annuity accumulates, compounding tax–deferred until the funds are withdrawn.

There are two types of annuities: fixed and variable. In a fixed annuity, the insurance company invests the funds in fixed–income investments, such as bonds and mortgages, and guarantees the principal and a minimum rate of return. The funds in a variable annuity are invested in stocks, bonds and mutual funds. Neither the principal nor minimum payout is guaranteed. Some companies allow you to split your investment between fixed and variable accounts.

When you want to start payouts, you have a number of choices. A straight-life annuity will pay periodic benefits for your lifetime—but with no payments to any beneficiary. A periodic annuity will pay benefits for only a specified number of years. If you die before the payout is finished, a beneficiary will continue to receive payments for the time specified. A joint–and–survivor payout will provide you with a specified payout, and upon your death, a reduced amount will go to a beneficiary for the remainder of his or her lifetime. The amount of the payout will depend on the payout option you select.

You can buy annuities with a single premium or through periodic installments. Insurance companies have minimum dollar investments for each. They also impose a penalty on early withdrawals from an annuity. The penalty is usually 6 or 7 percent in the first year; it then reduces by 1 percent per year until there is no penalty.

Annuities are one of the few tax–deferred investments you can find today. Many people have taken a closer look at annuities since Black Monday (October 19, 1987).

High–risk investments

If you do not need current income and if you can take some high risks, consider investments in some of the more esoteric forms: precious metals (gold or silver), coins, diamonds and other precious gems, stamp collections, art objects. If you want to become really sophisticated, get together with your stockbroker and find out about puts and calls, buying and selling on options, commodities, futures contracts, oil and gas exploration, real estate. There are countless ways to

make—and lose—money through investments. Just be sure you know your situation and your objectives before you put any money into the more aggressive and speculative investments.

Avoiding investment mistakes

Some basic tips:

1. Make sure you have a solid foundation. Is money put away somewhere for a rainy day? For a specific goal? Do you have enough life insurance? A positive cash flow? Do you already have the dream house?

2. Work out an investment plan. Decide on middle– and long–range investment objectives. Do you want to accumulate a down payment for a house, in a hurry? Are you looking for security over the long term? Are you going into the market on a long–term or short–term basis? Do you want (or expect) to "make a killing"? Are you *willing* to invest for the long term, and do you have the patience to do so?

3. Know where you stand financially. Review your situation regularly. Do a Net Worth Statement and a cash–flow analysis.

4. Understand your risk factor and your risk temperature. Don't invest in anything that keeps you awake at night. Know yourselves—and how much risk you are willing to take.

5. Be informed. Read financial publications. Know what you are buying. Ask educated questions (they won't be educated questions unless you keep yourself informed) of a broker or an investment adviser. Take charge. Formulate your own plan—with advice.

6. Be ready to make changes. Remember—you are not married to any stock. If you have a loser, admit you made a mistake and get out. As your needs and objectives change, reevaluate your investments. *Never* get sentimental about a stock.

7. Don't expect miracles. There aren't any. It is easy to talk about gains. You will have losses, too. Remember—there is a trade–off between risk and return—if you want a high return, you have to take a high risk.

8. No one type of investment works best all the time.

9. To avoid reversals, you must diversify. Do not put all your eggs in one basket.
10. Think *liquidity* at all times. Know what you will sell to get cash if you have to.

IRA (Individual Retirement Account)

Before 1982, only workers who had no pension or profit–sharing plans at their places of work were eligible to establish IRAs. From 1982 through 1986, anyone who had earned income could contribute to an IRA and deduct the amount from his or her Federal income taxes.

IRAs are still available for everyone, but the Tax Reform Act of 1986 limited the tax deductibility of the contribution. Today you can claim your IRA contribution as a deduction if:

1. You are not covered by an employer–sponsored retirement plan, or married to anyone who is, regardless of income.
2. You are covered by a retirement plan but your income is below a certain amount. If you are a couple whose adjusted gross income is $40,000 or less or a single with adjusted gross income of $25,000 or less, you may still take the full deduction, even if you are covered by a retirement plan.

You can take partial deductions if you're a couple with income between $40,000 and $50,000 or a single who earns between $25,000 and $35,000. Basically, you lose $200 of deductibility for each $1,000 of income over the $40,000 as a couple or $25,000 as a single. Thus, if you're a married couple with an adjusted gross income of $42,000, you may deduct $1,600 of your $2,000 IRA contribution.

Many people question whether they should still contribute to an IRA if they can't deduct it. It is important to remember that earnings on all contributions are tax–deferred. In other words, you do not pay any income tax on the earnings or capital appreciation until you start to withdraw the funds at retirement.

How much may you put in each year? Up to $2,000 (or up to 100 percent of your *taxable* income—whichever is less). If husband and wife are both wage earners, they may contribute up to $4,000. If one spouse is not working, the other may contribute to an account in the name of the non–working spouse, up to a total of $2,250 in both accounts (or up to 100 percent of the compensation of the working spouse, whichever is less). If you are doing this, you may divide the contributions between your two accounts as you choose, but no more than $2,000 may be contributed to the account of either one in any single year.

You do not *have* to put in $2,000 every year. You may put in as much as you feel comfortable with. But it is important to avoid, if possible, taking money out of an IRA before you reach the age of 59 1/2, because you will have to pay a penalty of 10 percent on the amount you withdraw. So if you take out, say, $2,000, you will not only have to pay a tax on that amount (the tax you were sheltered from when you put the money into the IRA in the first place), but you will also have to pay a $200 penalty.

As a matter of fact, you shouldn't let the penalty deter you from saving for retirement or starting an IRA. There will come a break–even point—the point at which the penalty paid for early withdrawal will even out against the other forms of investment that are not tax–sheltered.

By the way, while you are thinking ahead, let me make it clear that you do not *have* to take out your IRA savings when you reach 59 1/2. But you must begin to withdraw the money by the time you are 70 1/2 or face some stiff penalties. (But that's a long way off, of course, and the penalties could change by then—look how bank deregulation in 1983 reduced the "stiff penalties" on cashing certificates of deposit.)

How is the money paid out to you? You get three choices:

1. You may take the entire sum in one lump payment (presumably you would then invest it elsewhere—or would you simply enjoy a six–month trip around the world?).
2. You may decide to receive it in regular installments over a fixed period. The period is limited to your life expectancy or the averaged combined life expectancy of you and your spouse.
3. You may choose an annuity that will make regular payments for as long as you or your spouse live.

What about taxes on the money you put in the IRA? When you start making withdrawals, the money you take out is taxed as ordinary income. If you take it all out in one lump sum, you will be taxed in that year on the total amount.

What happens to the money if you die? The balance in your account can be rolled over by the surviving spouse into his or her own IRA.

Must you always keep the money in the same IRA account? No. You may move it to another bank, if you wish, or to a different kind of account—either by direct transfer or by rollover. In a direct transfer, you never gain possession of the money during the transfer. It goes directly from one trustee to another. For example, you may ask your bank to transfer the funds directly to a mutual fund. In a rollover, on the other hand, you actually get a check or cash from the bank. You must then deposit it in another IRA account within 60 days or pay tax on it as ordinary income and pay the 10 percent penalty.

Note: After any rollover, you must wait at least 12 months before you may do it again; direct transfers, however, are not limited to any waiting period.

Does it make any difference when you make your contributions to your IRA? You bet. The earlier in the year, the better. If you deposit money in January that money and the interest it immediately starts to earn are tax deferred—protected from any tax—for that entire year. And your money has that much more time to grow, because the interest starts from day one. If, on the other hand, you put the money into a regular savings account or money market fund, waiting until before the April 15 deadline the following year to move it into an IRA, the interest it earns will be taxable.

The difference an IRA can make

If you put the maximum of $2,000 into an IRA every year for 10 years and it earns 10 percent, you will have about $35,062 in the account at the end of 10 years. If you put the same amount, at the same interest, in an account where you pay taxes on the interest, assuming that you are in the 25 percent tax bracket, you will have about $23,000 in 10 years. The higher your tax bracket, the less you will have.

Does it make any difference *where* you invest the funds?

Yes. IRA funds can go into almost any type of account. Banks, insurance companies, brokerage firms, and mutual funds are all clamoring for your money. So you need to look at all aspects of your situation and make a decision. How long do you plan to make contributions? What type of risk are you willing to take? At your age you can probably afford to take some risks, knowing that if there are losses you will have time to make up the difference. How much can you contribute each year? Some IRAs allow you to make small or frequent contributions, while others do not. While you do not have to contribute every year, it's a good habit to get into.

Here are some of the ways you can set up an IRA. Before deciding on any one, you should get specific information from the institution you are considering.

1. *Banks.* Most offer a variety of options patterned on those offered by the conventional certificate of deposit. The options involve the kind of interest, the amount of interest, and the length of the certificate. Some offer variable or floating interest; others do not, so you should compare interest rates offered by different institutions. Most banks will let you open an IRA with as little as $100.

2. *Credit unions.* Most credit unions design their IRA's to fit the size and nature of the union. The rate of interest is set by the board of directors. Your initial deposit may be quite low, and deposits may be deducted directly from your paycheck if your employer is willing to extend such a benefit—a real convenience for you.

3. *Insurance companies.* An IRA set up with an insurance company is an annuity. A minimum rate of interest will be fixed through the years, possibly high in the early years, then lower as time goes on. You may have to pay an annual fee and sales costs, with a sizeable penalty if you withdraw the money prematurely (probably even higher if you withdraw in the very early years of the policy).

4. *Mutual funds.* In this form of IRA you buy shares in a pool of money that is invested in securities chosen by professional money managers. In some mutual funds, your IRA is in a money market fund, where the investment is in short–term securities and the rate of return

varies daily. In others, the investment is in stocks and bonds, some in blue–chip companies, others in more risky, emerging companies. As you get older and your investment objectives change, you may move your IRA from one mutual fund to another. In order to do this, many people choose a company that operates several funds. Most funds require a minimum deposit—some as low as $100. Usually a yearly maintenance fee of $2 to $10 is charged.

5. *Investment brokers.* Here is where you will find the widest range of IRAs. You can build your own portfolio, using a "self–directed" plan: You make the decisions on investing in stocks, bonds, mutual funds or any other type of investment. Each time you buy or sell, you pay commissions. You will also have to pay some administrative fees. Most brokers expect you to invest the entire allowable $2,000 at one time, and it is really best to accumulate from $10,000 to $15,000 before you start to self–direct. Investing in securities, remember, means you risk loss. It is, however, the most flexible IRA route you can choose.

Think of the IRA as one of the foundation stones of financial fitness. It is never too soon to start an IRA. It means you are making a long–term commitment, but it is well worth it—especially in view of the current widespread concern over the future of Social Security.

And incidentally, don't think you *have* to start with the $2,000 maximum the law allows. Little IRA's grow up big. If you put in only $100 a year, you'll have $1,753 in 10 years, $6,300 in 20 years, $18,094 in 30 years. Or, $500 a year will produce $8,766 in 10 years, $31,501 in 20 years, and $90,472 in 30 years. Not bad, especially if inflation is kept under reasonable control.

Tips on IRAs

- Shop around. Financial institutions are in competition for your money.
- Check for payroll deduction plans. Your employer can make it easy to build your IRA. Weigh the relative safety of various plans.
- Compare the minimum amounts needed to open IRA accounts.
- Understand the kind of interest or other return that is offered. It makes a difference in the dollars coming to you later. Interest on $1,000 contributed every year at 9 percent will give you about $55,000 in 20 years. At 13 percent, you will get $91,000.
- Compare interest rates. They vary from locality to locality and from institution to institution. And they can change during the life of your IRA, so keep an eye on them over the years in case it becomes wise to make a direct transfer or a rollover.
- Keep an eye on the marketplace, too. Continue to study the options available so you can make informed decisions on transfers or rollovers.

Join—or form—an investment club

A great way to get yourselves educated about investments, with little risk, is to hook up with an investment club. Maybe talk with several other couples about forming a club if you don't already know of one. A stockbroker in your area will be glad to help you get started.

This is a way to get your feet wet even if you have only a small amount to invest. No one couple in your group would probably have enough money to make significant investments or attract the attention of a broker, but when you pool your resources your investment club will have enough. And you can make the meetings a social as well as educational event.

YOU AND THE LAW: WHO OWNS WHAT AND WHAT YOU'LL LEAVE BEHIND— YOUR WILL

13

"Husband and wife are one...and that one is the husband."

That is what common law once held. A woman lost not only her name but her financial identity when she married.

Marriage is a legal union recognized by society through the government. In the United States, each state government sets regulations on wedlock, applying considerations of what is called "public policy." Public policy can and does vary according to current understandings of what society wants or thinks is good for itself. Public policy changes as time goes by.

Take property rights. Until the mid–1800s, public policy decreed that women lost control over their property when they entered into wedlock. Then, late in the 19th century, the Married Women's Property Acts were passed, giving women the right to own property in their names even though they were married.

Only in very recent years have women retained their own names upon marriage. A separate legal identity was extremely rare for a woman.

Today the status of women is changing. It is common to read in a wedding announcement that "the bride will retain her own name." And for the past several generations women have been able to own property without their husbands' say–so.

Generally speaking, each spouse owns whatever he or she brings into the marriage. The man and the woman each have the right to buy or sell "separate property," or to borrow money against it. However, you can lose control of separate property. For instance, if you put your money into a joint bank account it is then presumed, in most states, to belong to both of you—and either of you can take it out of the account.

Community–property laws in nine states

In certain states, however, everything (or almost everything) is fifty–fifty. They have passed community property laws that say that all money and property—salaries and assets including real estate, furniture, books, or whatever— acquired during marriage are considered the joint community property of both husband and wife. The only exceptions are money and property acquired through inheritance or a gift from a third party. What's more, community property in these states does not carry the right of survivorship. When one spouse dies, the other does not automatically assume full ownership. Each spouse must make disposition of his or her half by a legal will. If there is no will, the laws of the state take over.

Which states have community–property laws? Arizona, California, Idaho, Louisiana, Nevada, New Mexico, Texas, Washington and Wisconsin. Their laws are not all the same, however, so it is important if you live in one of these states to know its particular community–property rules.

It is also possible for you to own community property in a state that does not have such laws. If you once lived in a community–property state and acquired property while there, it remains community property even after you have moved to a "common–law" state. The opposite is not true, however. If either of you owned property while living in a common–law state, and you move to a community–property state, the property does not become community property— worth knowing if either of you works for a big company that is likely to move you around from place to place as your career advances.

Four types of ownership

Whether you are acquiring a house, stocks, bonds, or a bank account, you have a choice, in all common–law states, of any of these four kinds of ownership:

1. *Separate.* Any individual, whether married or not, may hold title and full ownership. A spouse has no claim on the property. Upon death, it is passed on by the owner's will or by the state's intestate laws if there is no will.

2. *Joint tenant with right of survivorship.* Two or more people jointly hold title and ownership. On the death of any one of the joint tenants, that person's entire interest in the property passes automatically to the survivor or survivors. It does not take a will to make this happen. It is instant and automatic.

3. *Tenants by entirety.* This is a special form of joint ownership between husband and wife. It gives either tenant the right of survivorship upon the death of the other. But there is an important difference: This tenancy can be ended only by mutual consent or by the termination of the marriage. A joint tenancy with right of survivorship, on the other hand, can be ended by one of the tenants acting unilaterally.

4. *Tenants in common.* This form of ownership involves two or more tenants, each with some proportion of the ownership. Each may sell or donate his or her share, or dispose of it by will.

Which type of ownership is right for you, as a couple? You have to decide. Choosing the right one is important, for it can affect your future. The more property you own, the more attention you should pay to how it is owned. ***Note:*** You do not have to put all your property into the same type of ownership. Joint tenant with right of survivorship is an easy form and is, of course, the ultimate sign of togetherness.

Tip: If you are setting up Individual Retirement Accounts (IRAs), and if you are *both* working, you will want *separate* ownership rather than *spousal* or *joint* ownership. That way, acting as individuals, you can each put in up to $2,000 each year (as against a total of $2,250 yearly in a spousal account). Another example is the stock market. If you both want to invest in the market, do so under your separate names rather than buying any given stock jointly.

Advantages and disadvantages of joint ownership

You can get a nice cozy feeling of security from jointly owned property.

Its advantages include these:

- It passes immediately to the survivor, staying out of probate.
- It is easy to set up.
- It assures an inheritance for a spouse with no funds of his or her own, because jointly held property cannot be sold without the permission of the other spouse.
- It can eliminate ancillary probate (that is, probate in another state). This is important, for instance, if you own a vacation home in another state. Be sure the place is jointly held, in order to avoid probate fees.
- Creditors may not be able to seize jointly held property, unless the surviving spouse assumed liability. Again, each state has different laws.

You should also be aware of some disadvantages of jointly held property:

- Signatures of both spouses are needed in order to sell property. This can be a problem in a divorce situation or if one spouse is absent and has not given a power of attorney to the other.
- Either spouse can clean out a joint bank account.
- Jointly held property cannot be willed. Neither spouse has any say in how the surviving spouse is to dispose of property.
- It may be subject to gift taxes.
- In a large estate, when one spouse dies, jointly held property added to the surviving spouse's estate may swell it to too large a size, making it tax prone. By carefully planning while both spouses are living, wills can be drawn to pass certain property directly to the children or grandchildren.
- Accounts can be frozen by banks, preventing the survivor from using the money.

As your assets increase and you acquire a home, more furniture, cars, stocks and bonds and other investments, the question of who owns what will become more and more important. *Choosing the right kind of ownership can become difficult.* A lawyer or accountant who knows the federal and local estate and property laws will be able to help you make the right decisions.

You can change later

The way you set up ownership at the start of your marriage does not mean that everything is set in concrete. You can change later. Even the deed on your house can be changed. If one of you already owns a house, for example, you can make your spouse a joint owner when you marry.

Tip: Before making any change in the kind of ownership you are using, check the tax consequences. Talk with a lawyer or accountant who knows tax law and who can look at the specifics of your situation and tell you which kind of ownership gives you the greatest advantages.

Do we need wills?

You bet. If you have *anything* to leave behind—a single personal possession or only a few dollars—you want to make certain it will go where you want it to go after you die. And that is what a will is for. In most states, anyone who is at least 18 years old and of sound mind may make a will.

A will is your means of making decisions, putting them on paper, and seeing to it that the paper becomes a legal document that no one can argue about.

If you die without a will, you will be said to have died "intestate." The state in which you live immediately before death then becomes responsible for deciding who gets your property. Its decisions may or may not fit the ideas you had. The possibilities of inequities are great. For example, suppose you die and leave your spouse with small children. You would probably assume—and desire—that everything you owned would go to your spouse. But the state, under the law, might give your spouse only a little more than one half, with the rest left to your children. The state would also name guardians for any minor children—guardians you might never have wanted.

Your will gives you control not only over who gets what, but over how and when. It conserves and distributes your estate the way you want it done. It names guardians for children—the guardians the two of you have agreed on. (Nothing is worse than a family squabble over who is to take care of children; often a split occurs, with elderly grandparents taking charge and with the children enduring still another change of guardianship when the grandparents die.)

What is an "estate"?

Your estate is everything you own: your money, your house and land, all your worldly possessions. Estate planning is planning for what is to become of it all. It is really nothing more than caring for those who are likely to survive you. From reading this book and filling in its worksheets, you are already well on your way to estate planning, because:

- You have your papers and records in order.
- You know your assets and who owns what.
- You understand income and expenses.
- You know how much life insurance you have—and need.
- You know about your pension.

It will be important to review your will regularly, at least every five years. Here are some of the reasons why you may need to update it:

- the birth of a child
- the death of a beneficiary or of the executor (the person you have chosen to handle the details of the will when you die)
- marriage or divorce
- a move to a different state, where the laws may be different
- a major change in your financial circumstances
- new law affecting estates.

How is a will made?

A will is a formal document, and making it is a fairly formal procedure. The law will consider it to be an effective document only if it meets certain criteria.

- In most states, a will must be executed in writing.

- It must be signed by the person who is making the will.
- It must be attested by at least two witnesses who sign in the presence of the person making the will. (Your witnesses may be called upon to testify in court that they saw you sign the will.)

How long does a will last—and can it be changed?

A will is in effect until it is revoked. You can revoke your will at any time. If your marital state changes or you have a child (or legally adopt a child), your will is automatically revoked unless a provision is made to cover such an occurrence. Any such change in your circumstances, or any substantial change in your assets, should be your cue to see what changes must be made in your will. It can be changed any time, and as frequently as necessary.

Consult a lawyer

Even if you think you may not have enough worldly goods to justify making a will, look around you. Insurance policies, company benefits, your home, investments, household furnishings—all may add up to more of an estate than you thought you had.

Have an attorney draw up your will. A good lawyer will know the laws of your state, and will avoid problems that you might create by making your own homemade will. You can save your lawyer's time, and your own money, by doing the following:

- Have ready a list of your assets (from your Net Worth Statement).
- Choose an executor, a friend or relative whom you trust. This person will be fully responsible for seeing your will through probate and making sure your estate is disposed of properly. This person should live nearby. If he or she dies, you must revise your will to name another.
- Choose a guardian for your children. Guardians will be expected to provide proper care as well as manage money for the children. Before you name a guardian in your will, be sure you ask the prospective guardian if it is all right with him or her.
- Decide who is to get what from your estate.

- Use everyday English. Say what you mean. Mean what you say. Avoid ambiguities.

Ask your attorney to maintain the original signed copies of your will and your spouse's. Keep duplicate copies in your files at home and, for extra safety, in your safe–deposit box.

Probate—what's that all about?

Your estate is either of two types: *probate* and/or *taxable.* You may have an asset that is jointly owned and that does not go through the probate process. Yet it may be part of your taxable estate.

The function of probate court is to authorize and supervise the payment of funeral expenses, taxes, and debts owed by a person who dies, and to authorize the cost of administering the estate. Usually your executor is paid for handling your estate. The court then sees that any remaining property is distributed to the beneficiaries or to any others who are entitled to it.

The executor works under the supervision and scrutiny of the probate court. If you do not have a will, the court—acting on behalf of the state—will name an administrator.

This is the probate procedure:

1. Probating the will. Application is made for probate of the will, which is filed with the court and declared valid. The court approves the executor named in the will, or names an administrator.
2. Posting of a bond by the executor or administrator (unless your will waives the requirement). The amount of the bond will depend on the size of the estate.
3. Inventory of all assets that are owned in your name *alone.* This is needed to determine whether your estate is solvent. Assets must be evaluated. Appraisers will be called in to judge the value of real estate and certain collectibles such as coins, jewelry, and so on. An up–to–date Net Worth Statement can be a great aid at this point.
4. Advertising for claims against the estate. This is in case any unknown debts are "out there" somewhere. The notice will specify that all claims must be submitted within a stated period, otherwise they need not be honored. At the same time,

all recent and outstanding bills, such as funeral or medical expenses, are paid.
5. Filing of state and federal tax forms, as required by various laws, and payments of the taxes.
6. Final accounting and distribution of the remaining estate to those named in the will.

That is the probate procedure. It involves certain time limits set by state law (the inventory, for example, must be completed within a certain time). The entire procedure can take anywhere from nine months to two or three years, depending on the complexity of the will, size of the estate, and number of beneficiaries.

Note: Once a will has been probated, it is a matter of public record. That's why many people prefer to establish trusts for their beneficiaries; trusts are not made public.

Estate taxes

The Economic Recovery Act of 1981 provides an unlimited marital deduction, so there are no Federal estate taxes on the amount you leave to your spouse, no matter the size of your estate. However, some states do limit marital deductions, so you need to check on the law in the state where you live.

If the taxable estate is $600,000 or more, Federal estate taxes will be due on the death of the surviving spouse. This sounds like a lot, but as your assets grow you may find that your estate exceeds $600,000—especially when you add in such "hidden" assets as life insurance proceeds, pension or profit–sharing plans, company stock and employer-sponsored saving plans such as a 401(k).

The tax bite can be substantial—anywhere from 37 to 50 percent of your (or your spouse's) taxable estate.

Wills and estate planning

As your assets grow you will need to get into estate planning. Your will should be revised in conjunction with such plans. By developing the two together—will and estate plan—you and your lawyer can not only take care of the needs of your spouse and family, you can also take advantage of many ways to reduce or eliminate taxes and other expenses that could otherwise shrink your estate. Your will not only tells people what you want done with your assets, it also helps to preserve them.

How to choose professional advisers

The various aspects of your financial life will call for experts in various fields to give you advice. At one time or another you will need an attorney, an insurance agent, a real estate broker, an accountant, a financial planner, a stockbroker, a banker. But don't forget that within each of these professions there are specialists, just as there are within the medical profession. You wouldn't go to an ear, nose and throat doctor if you had a broken ankle. By the same token, the lawyer who handles the closing on your home may not be the right one to see when you want to draw your will or incorporate the business firm you are forming. So always seek the appropriate professional. See if he or she has the area of expertise you need. Ask people you know who are in your situation. See who they used, and how satisfied they were.

The most important thing is to feel comfortable with any professional you are using. You're going into a long–term relationship, so take your time, interview, ask questions, really get to know the individual.

It's important, too, to find professionals who understand your needs and objectives. Tell them your goals. Be open and honest. Recognize your own risk factors and let your advisers know what they are. And never be afraid to make a change if you are unhappy, feel you are not getting enough attention, or discover that you have been getting poor advice.

Above all, don't put yourself in the "I don't want to bother him/her with such a silly question" frame of mind. That, I have to tell you, is ridiculous. Your advisers are there to be bothered with any questions you have. In fact, you could pay very dearly for not having sought advice or taking bad advice. That's why it's important to be sure your adviser is a specialist in the subject you seek help with.

RECORD KEEPING

14

From reading all these chapters, you know that managing your money involves being able to prove what you spent, where you spent it, what you spent it for, how it improved or failed to improve your financial situation.

What you need for all this money management is *records*—not a mountain of paper, but a practical system for keeping track of financial matters and important papers related to them over a long period of time.

You should begin keeping records from the time of your first job on through your retirement years. The record keeping itself can be a simple file system of various papers, some items being permanent, some semipermanent, others temporary. For instance, obviously you keep an insurance policy on file as long as it is in force. You keep automobile papers as long as you own the car. You keep home improvement records until you sell the house and want to prove how much extra capital you have put into it over the years. You keep ordinary sales receipts and other income tax records for three years, until the statute of limitations runs out: An audit by the IRS may go back no

more than three years. However, you should keep your final IRS tax return for each year in a permanent file. It makes an excellent financial history.

A costly failing

Not having a good system of record keeping can be not only embarrassing but costly. The newly widowed woman who cannot find her husband's life insurance policies suffers embarrassment as well as grief. And you don't have to be newly widowed to lose money in another way. Banks regularly take out local newspaper advertisements to list the names and last known addresses of thousands of customers who have left accounts inactive for a specified period. If a bank fails to locate an owner of an account after placing such an advertisement, the unclaimed money goes to the state. Billions of dollars from bank accounts are held in state treasuries simply because no one can trace the assets to their rightful owners. If you move from state to state, as many couples do as a result of corporate relocations or when job opportunities open, you run the risk of forgetting to transfer an inactive savings account with you if you don't have a good system of record keeping.

By the same token, if you own a piece of property, move away, forget to tell the tax assessor where you have gone, and then fail to pay the taxes (people can and do forget such things—it happens in surprising numbers every year), the town may auction that parcel of land to the highest bidder—and keep the proceeds.

Some states exact a personal property tax on cars and boats. In our computer age, any state motor vehicle department can make a quick check on whether the tax has been paid on an automobile and will refuse to renew a car's registration if it has not. I had a client who sold his boat but did not keep the bill of sale. Months later the state demanded tax due on his boat. To prove he no longer owned the boat and therefore owed no tax, he had to trace the boat to a dealer in Florida and get another receipt.

Some people have had to reconstruct the history of an illness a year or more after they got well—because they didn't make medical records promptly and hang onto them. Since most doctors' offices ask for payment at the time of your visit and leave it up to you to handle major–medical and other insurance claims, it is important to make a habit of getting a photocopy of all receipts and claim forms, and filing all claims promptly.

Important: If your doctor (or hospital or diagnostic lab) is not paid at the time of your visit and you are then reimbursed by an insurance company (this is likely to happen with a group major–medical program where you work), be sure you pay the bill immediately when you get the money from the insurance company. If you spend that money on something else, saying "Oh, I'll take care of the doctor [or hospital or lab] later," you are giving yourself a habit that can only lead to problems.

You can replace many records. But it takes time, effort, and postage. Stock certificates are a good example. If you own more than one or two, make an accurate list: by name, number of shares, purchase price, and date of purchase. If you should have to compile such a list after your certificates have been lost, stolen, or destroyed in a fire, it can be horren-

dous—and the result may not be complete. Before any company will issue a replacement certificate, you will have to sign an affidavit that the certificate was destroyed, then put up a surety bond—which can cost as much as three percent of the current market price.

What goes to the bank, what stays home?

Where should you keep important papers and records? Some belong in a safe–deposit box in a bank. Others can be at home in a sensible file—in a safe place.

Papers that are difficult to replace should be in the safe–deposit box. These include:

Birth certificates
Stock certificates
Marriage certificate
Citizenship papers
Bonds
Certificate of title for an automobile
Real estate deeds
Copy of will (but not the original)
Divorce decree
Death certificates
Passports
Discharge from military service
Veterans Administration papers
Adoption papers
Contracts
Household inventory (including photographs for appraisal purposes).

What about life insurance policies—and why not put the original copy of your will in the safe–deposit box? Because in most states when the owner, or joint owner, of a safe–deposit box dies, the bank seals the box until all tax and legal matters are taken care of. Access is granted only when the bank receives legal permission, and then in the presence of an authorized person. A life insurance company will not pay a claim until the policy is surrendered. The probation of a will cannot begin until the last will is presented to the probate court. Thus, everything is held up if legal permission to open a safe deposit box has to be obtained.

The best place to keep your life insurance policies is at home. The best place to keep the original copy of your will is in the files of the attorney who drew it up.

Fill out the worksheets at the end of this chapter: XII, **Personal Information**; XIII, **Personal Contacts**; XIV, **Record Keeping**; and XV, **Location of Other Important Papers**.

Tip: It is better to jot down too much than too little. Don't be afraid to put in details. Some details may seem obvious. But remember that they will not be obvious to anyone who must track down all this information if you're not on hand to supply it. And lawyers can tell you how much they are paid to take care of "nuisance" details that could easily have been ready in a file.

When you have filled out these sheets, make duplicates. Give a set to someone else to keep for you—someone who will understand the method of your madness.

File—and throw out

What counts is not what your filing system looks like. What counts is how well you have organized it. For some, it may be a collection of shoe boxes. For others, it may be file cabinets with suspension drawers on ball bearings. The key is to get into the habit of filing those papers that are important and *throwing out* those that are not.

Your permanent home file should include:

Annuities
Automobile insurance
Bankbooks and statements
Children's records
Credit histories
Disability insurance policy
Educational records (for each member of the family)
Employment history
Federal income tax returns
Gift tax returns
Health insurance coverage and policies
Health records
Home improvements
Homeowner's insurance

Household inventory (with receipts and appraisals)
Insurance policies (if not filed under subject headings, such as automobile, medical, and so on)
IRA (individual retirement account) or 401(k)
Keogh plan
Life insurance policies
List of important advisers
Loan applications
Loans
Medical insurance
Medicare policy
Mutual funds
Paid bills
Pension and profit–sharing plans
Property–tax bills and receipts
Real estate investments
Social Security earnings records
Social Security numbers
State income tax returns
Stock options
Stock and bond record book
Warranties and guarantees
Wills (file signed original with attorney)

Records of stocks, bonds and home improvements

With these items, it is important to know—maybe years from now—what you paid. This is strictly a matter of keeping good records for tax purposes.

If you are into stocks and bonds enough to keep a record book on them, use a different colored pen for each year in which you have stock transactions. If you are using blue ink for this year, for instance, you will know that all blue ink items that are sold must be included in this year's tax return.

It is important to have a record of when you bought a particular stock, and at what price. Save trade confirmations and dividend–reinvestment statements from your mutual funds. When you sell it, it will be necessary to figure out the gain or loss on the sale. Even if many years have passed between the purchase and the sale, you will have to pay a tax on any profit. Many people overpay on their taxes because they have no idea how to figure out the cost basis of an investment.

Save all your statements from your Individual Retirement Accounts, especially those identifying non–deductible contributions. If you don't have verification of the amount and date of a particular contribution, you could end up paying taxes when you make withdrawals from your non–deductible IRAs.

The same is true of your house or condominium. When you sell, you must pay a tax on the profit (that is, the difference between the original purchase price and the sale price). But the cost of every permanent improvement made over the years may be added to the original purchase price: landscaping, for instance, or converting a garage to a playroom; installing insulation and other energy–saving devices; the addition of a building, swimming pool, deck, or patio; or doing anything else that added value to the house. An accurate record of bills paid and canceled checks will be invaluable when the house is sold.

Save receipts from expensive items such as jewelry, furniture and other collectibles. You might need them for an insurance claim in case of damage, loss or theft.

Tip: Before you move out, take pictures in and around the house. When you prepare your tax return they will jog your memory. You'll be surprised how many improvements you will see in those photos.

Files for income tax returns

A continuing file related to your annual income tax returns is vitally important. If the IRS decides to audit your return any year, the burden of proof will be on you. An accordion file of canceled checks, organized by categories, will help you with tax returns—as well as with budget planning. Filing categories include such items as:

Automobile expenses
Bills from specific stores
Children's expenses
Clothing
Contributions
Education
Entertainment and recreation
Household expenses (maintenance)
Household purchases (major)
Insurance premiums
Medical and dental expenses

Mortgage payments
Taxes (real estate and personal property)
Utilities

With this file at your fingertips, you can tackle a new year's budgeting and your end–of–year tax return with confidence in your accuracy. And you can throw out many bills. Do just that. Keep only what you need as evidence for tax purposes.

Make yourself do this kind of housekeeping at least annually

Tip: One good system is to keep two sets of files: one for tax–deductible items, the other for major personal financial items—some of which may be tax–related. Tax–deductible items would include expenses for business entertainment (if they were not reimbursed by your employer) or subscriptions to professional publications. This file would also include income from free–lance or moonlighting jobs as well as from your regular job, and expenses for major home improvements. The other file would contain your records on insurance, investments, and job benefits where you work.

If the IRS audits you

The IRS does not understand the words "I can't find it." If you want to prove you made an expenditure, you must bring in the proof.

In fact, the IRS considers you guilty until you prove yourself innocent. It is permitted by law to audit you any time up to three years from the date you filed a return. In addition, if it thinks there is reason to charge you with fraud or gross negligence, it may audit you at a later date.

Once the three years have passed, you should *throw out* most of your canceled checks and documentation, keeping only those items that have to do with possible future capital gains tax information, such as home improvements or the purchase of collectibles and stocks and bonds.

What can you do if you are called in for an audit?

Be prepared. Your notice from the IRS will indicate the sections of your tax return that it wants to check on. The letter will tell you to call for an appointment, probably at the nearest IRS office. If your return was prepared by an accountant, contact him or her and see if the accountant will go in your place. (Be sure to find out if there is an additional fee for this service and decide whether to pay it and be represented or, at least for the first meeting, to go by yourself and find out what's on the IRS's mind.) Take with you—or send with the accountant—all the bills and canceled checks relating to the particular items the IRS has said it wants to check on.

Tip: In an IRS meeting, keep your eyes and ears open and your mouth closed as much as possible. Do not volunteer information. Answer only the questions you are asked. Do not chitchat. Control the natural tendency, in a nervous situation, to babble. Concentrate on counting the holes in the ceiling tiles, if you must, but fight the urge to blurt out something you may regret. You can let out your primal scream when you get out of the office.

Record keeping has its emotional aspects. Being able to put your hands on the right piece of paper at the right time is the greatest relief ever devised for an anxiety attack. If you have been wise enough to let someone else in on the secret of your method of record keeping, you will be in much better shape during an unexpected period of transition or emotional turmoil.

VALERIE AND JAMES McQUARTER KEEP METICULOUS RECORDS

They must. Their income is almost entirely from self-employment. No employer withholds money from their pay to send in to the IRS or to Social Security. They must keep an accurate record of every penny they earn. "I keep a calendar on my desk to mark down income from every gig we play," says Valerie. "On any day that either of us receives a check, I note the amount right on that day on the calendar. I also put it down in a book, so we can double-check. We fell into this system when we first started, and now it is habit."

"We pay all expenses for our business either by check on the spot or by charging them and paying by check later," says James. "Then we file the bills according to categories in an accordion file."

The McQuarters can watch their total income and the expenses incurred in earning it and know where they stand at any time. Because no tax money is withheld by those who hire them, the two musicians have to estimate their income taxes four times a year and send payments in to the IRS. Then, when they do their tax return, they file a Schedule C (Profit or Loss from Business or Profession). The profit (or loss) shown on Schedule C is entered on Form 1040's line 12. Because they have no Social Security payments deducted for them, they also fill out Schedule SE, which calculates the Social Security payment based on the profit from their profession.

Worksheet XII: The Bucks
Personal Information

Yourself:

1. Name __Patrick Buck__   Address __140 Rolling Lane__
   City/State __Trumbull, CT.__   Telephone Number __(203) 299-9555__
   Place of Birth __Minneapolis__   Date of Birth __5/5/55__
   Social Security # __000-50-8255__   Marital Status __Married__

2. Spouse's Name __Karen__   Address __Same as above__
   City/State _____   Telephone # _____
   Place of Birth __Des Moines, Iowa__   Date of Birth __7/23/56__
   Social Security # __500-40-6666__

3. Children:

Name	1 Landon	2 Megan	3	4
Address				
City/State				
Telephone				
Place of Birth	Omaha, NE	Des Moines, Iowa		
Date of Birth	1985	1988		
Social Security #				
Marital Status				

4. Parents
   Name __Joan & Jim Buck__   Address __4100 Town Ave.__
   City/State __St. Louis, Mo.__   Telephone # __(314) 592-6000__
   Place of Birth __St. Louis__   Date of Birth __10/12/30 Mother__
   Mother's maiden name __Smith__   __7/13/29 Father__

5. Spouse's Parents
   Names __Ellen & John Higgins__   Address __8200 Corn Dr.__
   City/State __Des Moines, Iowa__   Telephone __(515) 243-3480__
   Place of Birth __Des Moines__   Date of Birth __8/15/28 Mother__
   Mother's Maiden Name __Hudson__   __10/17/27 Father__

Next of Kin:
Name __Tom Buck__   Relationship __Brother__
Address __1800 Beacon St., Boston, MA__   Telephone # __(617) 437-9346__

Neighbor or Close Friend
Name __Martha & Fred Horn__   Address __147 Rolling Lane__
City/State __Trumbull, CT.__   Telephone __(203) 374-5141__

Worksheet XIII: The Bucks
Personal Contacts

	NAME	ADDRESS	TELEPHONE NUMBER
Attorney	Jack Miller	Bridgeport, CT.	(203)882-4000
Accountant	Myron Denn	Bridgeport, CT.	(203)681-2121
Clergyman	Rev. William Ryan	First Church	(203)681-4334
Stockbroker			
Physician	Dr. J. Green	Trumbull, CT.	(203)681-2201
Trust Officer			
Banker	Julia Rivers	Trumbull, CT.	(203)374-5141
Life Insurance Agent	Elaine Laper	Bridgeport, CT.	(203)681-4112
Other Insurance Agents			
Homeowner	Don Hill	Trumbull, CT.	(203)681-4112
Automobile	Don Hill	Trumbull, CT.	(203)681-4112
Medical	at work		
Disability	at work		
Executor of Estate	Tom Buck	Boston, MA.	(617)437-9346
Financial Planner			
Others			

Worksheet XIV: The Bucks
RECORD KEEPING

1. CHECKING ACCOUNTS, SAVINGS ACCOUNTS, CREDIT UNION ACCOUNTS, OTHER CASH ACCOUNTS

Name of Institution	Type and # of Account	Interest Rate	Current Balance	Owned By	Location of Checkbook or Passbooks
State Bank	checking 174151	5.5	1,500	Joint	desk
ABC Bank	checking 44111	5.5	500	Karen	
City	checking 771416	5.5	850	Pat	

2. MONEY MARKET FUNDS, CERTIFICATES OF DEPOSIT, TREASURY BILLS AND NOTES

Name of Institution	Type and # of Account	Maturity Date	Amount Invested	Interest Rate	Owned by	Location of Passbooks
State Bank	money 174111		15,000	7.5	joint	desk
			TOTAL			

3. SECURITIES

Stocks & Mutual Funds:

Number of Shares	Company	Date Purchased	Cost	Current Market Value	Owned By	Location of Stock Certificate	Annual Income

TOTAL:

Bonds: Corporate & Municipal

Face Amount	Company	Purchase Date	Maturity Date	Total Cost	Interest Rate	Current Market Value	Owned by	Location of Book	Annual Income

4. REAL ESTATE (RESIDENCE, RECREATIONAL, INCOME PROPERTY)

Location: 1. Trumbull   2.   3.
Date Purchased   6/88
Cost   250,000
Current Market Value   265,000

5. LIFE INSURANCE

	1.	2.	3.	4.
Insured	Patrick	Patrick	Karen	
Company	World	Friend Life	State Life	
Type of Policy	Group Term	Term	Group Term	
Number of Policy	456 19987	789-114-12	244-113-46	
Face Amount	$120,000	$100,000	$55,000	
Owner	Patrick	Patrick	Karen	
Beneficiary	Karen	Karen	Patrick	
Cash Value				
Amount Borrowed Out				
Location of Policy				

6. ANNUITIES, PENSIONS, PROFIT SHARING PLANS, INDIVIDUAL RETIREMENT ACCOUNTS

Description	Participant	Company or Institution	Benefits	Present Value
401(k)	Patrick			$63,500
IRA's	Patrick			$12,000
IRA's	Karen			$5,000

7. BUSINESS INTERESTS

Company Name	Type of Business	Percentage of Ownership	Value of Your Interest

8. CREDIT OBLIGATIONS

Real Estate (Residence, Recreational, Income Property)

	1.	2.	3.
Mortgage Holder	State Bank		
Mortgage Balance	$198,000		
Interest Rate	7.75%		
Monthly Payment	$1,608		

Other Debt Obligations (automobile loans, education loans, life insurance loans, home improvement loans, etc.)

Lender	Type of Loan	Interest Rate	Balance Due	Monthly Payment	Co-signer
ABC	Auto	13	11,500	265	
XYZ	Auto	15	2,000	214	

Credit Cards:

Name of Card	Number of card	Balance Due
Visa - Patrick	443-15-5555	250
Master Card - Karen	B33-45-6666	750
American Express - Patrick	15-1400-5168	1,250
Bloomingdales	221-44-66	250

Worksheet XV: The Bucks
LOCATION OF OTHER IMPORTANT PAPERS

Homeowner's Insurance _desk file_

Name of Company _Tower Insurance_   Policy Number _0998-82-02_

Automobile Insurance _desk file_

Name of Company _Tower Insurance_   Policy Number _9718-41-3867_

Medical Insurance _at work_

Name of Company _The Blues_   Policy Number _91156899-1_

Type of Policy _Major-Medical_

Location of card _wallet_   Group Number _____

Disability Insurance _____

Name of Company _____   Policy Number _____

Last Will _with Lawyer_

Codicils _____

Birth Certificates _safe-deposit box_

Mortgage Papers or Lease _safe-deposit box_

Deeds to Real Estate _safe-deposit box_

Titles to Automobiles _with bank until loan paid off_

Military Discharge Papers _____

Citizenship Papers _____

Divorce Decree _____

Social Security Cards _wallet_

Income Tax Returns _desk file_

Worksheet XII: Yours
PERSONAL INFORMATION

Yourself:

1. Name_____ Address_____

   City/State_____ Telephone Number_____

   Place of Birth_____ Date of Birth_____

   Social Security #_____ Marital Status_____

2. Spouse's Name_____ Address_____

   City/State_____ Telephone #_____

   Place of Birth_____ Date of Birth_____

   Social Security #_____

3. Children:

Name	1	2	3	4
Address				
City/State				
Telephone				
Place of Birth				
Date of Birth				
Social Security #				
Marital Status				

4. Parents

   Name_____ Address_____

   City/State_____ Telephone #_____

   Place of Birth_____ Date of Birth_____

   Mother's maiden name_____

5. Spouse's Parents

   Names_____ Address_____

   City/State_____ Telephone_____

   Place of Birth_____ Date of Birth_____

   Mother's Maiden Name_____

   Next of Kin:

   Name_____ Relationship_____

   Address_____ Telephone #_____

   Neighbor or Close Friend

   Name_____ Address_____

   City/State_____ Telephone_____

Worksheet XIII: Yours
Personal Contacts

	NAME	ADDRESS	TELEPHONE NUMBER
Attorney			
Accountant			
Clergyman			
Stockbroker			
Physician			
Trust Officer			
Banker			
Life Insurance Agent			
Other Insurance Agents			
Homeowner			
Automobile			
Medical			
Disability			
Executor of Estate			
Financial Planner			
Others			

Worksheet XIV: Yours
RECORD KEEPING

1. CHECKING ACCOUNTS, SAVINGS ACCOUNTS, CREDIT UNION ACCOUNTS, OTHER CASH ACCOUNTS

Name of Institution	Type and # of Account	Interest Rate	Current Balance	Owned By	Location of Checkbook or Passbooks

TOTAL

2. MONEY MARKET FUNDS, CERTIFICATES OF DEPOSIT, TREASURY BILLS AND NOTES

Name of Institution	Type and # of Account	Maturity Date	Amount Invested	Interest Rate	Owned by	Location of Passbooks

TOTAL

3. SECURITIES

Stocks & Mutual Funds:

Number of Shares	Company	Date Purchased	Cost	Current Market Value	Owned By	Location of Stock Certificate	Annual Income

Bonds: Corporate & Municipal

Face Amount	Company	Purchase Date	Maturity Date	Total Cost	Interest Rate	Current Market Value	Owned by	Location of Book	Annual Income

TOTAL:

4. REAL ESTATE (RESIDENCE, RECREATIONAL, INCOME PROPERTY)

Location: 1. _____ 2. _____ 3. _____

Date Purchased

Cost

Current Market Value

5. LIFE INSURANCE

	1.	2.	3.	4.
Insured				
Company				
Type of Policy				
Number of Policy				
Face Amount				
Owner				
Beneficiary				
Cash Value				
Amount Borrowed Out				
Location of Policy				

6. ANNUITIES, PENSIONS, PROFIT SHARING PLANS, INDIVIDUAL RETIREMENT ACCOUNTS

Description	Participant	Company or Institution	Benefits	Present Value

7. BUSINESS INTERESTS

Company Name	Type of Business	Percentage of Ownership	Value of Your Interest

8. CREDIT OBLIGATIONS

Real Estate (Residence, Recreational, Income Property)

	1.	2.	3.
Mortgage Holder			
Mortgage Balance			
Interest Rate			
Monthly Payment			

Other Debt Obligations (automobile loans, education loans, life insurance loans, home improvement loans, etc.)

Lender	Type of Loan	Interest Rate	Balance Due	Monthly Payment	Co-signer

Credit Cards:

Name of Card	Number of card	Balance Due

Worksheet XV: Yours
LOCATION OF OTHER IMPORTANT PAPERS

Homeowner's Insurance _____

    Name of Company _____ Policy Number _____

Automobile Insurance _____

    Name of Company _____ Policy Number _____

Medical Insurance _____

    Name of Company _____ Policy Number _____

    Type of Policy _____

    Location of card _____ Group Number _____

Disability Insurance _____

    Name of Company _____ Policy Number _____

Last Will _____

Codicils _____

Birth Certificates _____

Mortgage Papers or Lease _____

Deeds to Real Estate _____

Titles to Automobiles _____

Military Discharge Papers _____

Citizenship Papers _____

Divorce Decree _____

Social Security Cards _____

Income Tax Returns _____

YOUR OWN BALANCE SHEET

15

If you have read this far and filled in the worksheets, I think by now you have gained a strong sense of the financial fitness you can attain in your marriage. I like to think of it, as I have referred to it frequently in these pages, as a financial partnership—a closer partnership than you will ever find in the usual business partnership because it involves all the fun and excitement and rewards of building your lives together…sharing in working out goals and solving problems and creating a lifestyle and a family.

At the outset, I said I wrote this book because I was sure your generation wants to know how to manage money—in a way that earlier generations never knew. Yours is a generation that wants to see things as they are, tackle problems head–on, shoulder responsibility. You want to *manage*. And you want to keep in shape (the recent boom in physical fitness and exercise gear alone should prove that point!).

Let's take just a couple of pages for a summary and review of what's involved in maintaining your balance sheet on your financial partnership.

1. Have you set your goals?

Having sat down and figured out what are the most important short–range and long–range goals for each of you, have you reached agreement on priorities? This is important, remember, as the foundation for all your financial planning and management. Your goals evolve out of your own personal value systems. A frank analysis of your values—of what constitutes ego fulfillment for each of you—can be tremendously helpful in putting your goals in order. And it can help you reach real understanding of one another.

2. Who's managing—and how?

Have you put your heads together and figured out who's going to pay for what…how you are going to set up checking and savings accounts…which of you seems to be the better money handler, at least for now? This gets you into deciding whether to maintain separate checking accounts and a household account, and takes you right into the realm of your budget—the real key to how to manage your money right down to the last penny you spend for popcorn at the movies.

This is where you set up your disciplines—the regular habits you will follow as you proceed along the road map laid out by your budget. Here I trust that you have thought of—and put down on your worksheets—every item of income (or receivables) and every item of expense that come in and go out for each of you.

Don't forget that you are also setting up your fixed expenses and your flexible expenses so you can control funds held in reserve for each—and be sure your savings include regular monthly amounts needed to reach specific goals.

3. Raising children

Are you ready to face the financial realities of raising children? Have you fully grasped the idea (I must admit, it's hard for *me* to grasp!) that if you invite a baby into the world it could cost you as much as a quarter of a million dollars to see that child through college at age 22? That calls for plenty of planning by your financial partnership to see that there will be everything from rattles to ballet slippers to summer camp to braces and textbooks. (And all of it worth it for the joy the kids will give you.)

4. Worked out your net worth?

This is really what gets you down to the nitty–gritty, so I hope you have very conscientiously analyzed the value of your tangible assets and listed every single liability you can think of to give yourselves a true picture of where you stand. If you have done that, you should have a good sense of security—from knowing you have a positive net worth, or from discovering you have a negative net worth and realizing you must do something about it.

5. Credit and creditors

Is credit a problem? Have you found it hard to get credit cards—and have you used the tips I've suggested to see if you can get credit. Or—on the contrary—have you found it easy to let credit card charges mount up, until suddenly you're over your heads in debt? If you have worked out your debt ratio

and analyzed your situation, you may need to kick the spending habit for a while. Check back on that chapter and make sure things are under control

If you are repaying a student loan, are you taking advantage of your Sallie Mae options?

6. What about insurance and job?

Have you checked your personnel office at work on retirement benefits? On insurance coverage and possible choices from a "cafeteria" plan so that you and your spouse don't get duplicate coverage but do get coverage from one of your employers that you can't get from the other? Are you into two IRAs—one for each of you if you are both working, or a full IRA and a spousal IRA if one is not working?

How about insurance? Are you covered in all risk areas—life insurance, homeowner's, disability, major–medical, hospital/surgical/medical, automobile, umbrella liability? If you are working on any of these, don't forget to shop around. And don't forget to plan on reevaluating your coverage and needs at least every couple of years—more often if your family grows or your situation changes.

7. The roof, the market

If you're looking at the possibility of owning a home, have you done the homework to figure out how large a down payment you can afford, how long a mortgage you should sign up for, how large a monthly payment you can handle? Have you reviewed condo versus house and lot versus mobile home? Are you armed for dealing with bank talk about ARM (adjustable–rate mortgage)?

One of the most important considerations is the tax saving you will gain as a homeowner. If details on that are not clear, be sure to go back and review pages 87–96.

As to the stock market, remember that investing in the market is not something you enter into lightly. It comes *after* many other things: your solid basic savings, your emergency fund, your careful management of credit cards, your cautious analysis—*together*—of whether you have reached a point where you can assume the risks that come with investing.

8. *Got the records under control?*

If you have set up a good records system from the start of your marriage, you are way ahead. Good record keeping proves its worth over and over. Records are vital for budgeting, for seeing where you must shift the weight a little, change emphasis, cut expenses or increase them. You cannot create your budget road map without good records.

I hope you will use this book not only as a workbook but as a ready reference. Reread it now and then and redo the worksheets maybe once a year or every couple of years. It will help you to keep control—to *manage*, as I said at the outset, to take charge and keep charge of your finances. The more you work over your figures and understand them, the more comfortable you will be and the more your financial partnership will prosper. It will be financially fit.

A couple couldn't ask for more than that.

INDEX

policy, 114; universal life, 99; variable life, 99; whole or straight-life, 98-99

Interest on savings accounts, 120

Internal Revenue Service (IRS), 142

Investing, 119-131; annuities, 127-128; corporate bonds, 123; government savings bonds, 122-123; government securities, 122; high-risk, 128; mortgage-backed securities, 123-124; mutual funds, 125-127; objectives, 121; the stock market, 124; tax-exempt bonds, 123; zero-coupon bonds, 124

Investment clubs, 131

Investments for children, 28

J

Joint ownership, 135

L

Law, 133-138; community property, 134

Liabilities, 57

Loans, 69

M

Marriage as financial partnership, 2, 9

McQuarters, Valerie and James, 6; budget, 37-38; day-care, 22; insurance, 111; net worth, 57; pregnancy during self-employment, 20; record-keeping, 143

Money, 2-4; preserving and protecting, 3-4; management and children, 1-2; managing, 15- 17

Mortgage: assumable, 92; balloon, 92; fixed-rate, 91; graduated payment, 92; renegotiable-rate, 92; rollover, 92; variable-rate, 9, 1-92

N

Net worth, 55-56

New York Stock Exchange, 124

Nichols, Jeanne and Eric, 5, 13; budget, 38; computer, 17; credit, 70; mortgage, 93-94

P

Probate, 137

R

Record-keeping, 16, 139-157

S

Safe-deposit box, 140

Savings: accounts, 119-120; certificates of deposit, 120; compound interest chart, 121; difference between saving and investing, 119; fixed expense, as, 36; money market account, 120; passbook, 120; risks in investing, 121; time deposits, 120

Savings certificates, deregulation of fixed-term, 10

Savings and loan associations, 68

Small-loan companies, 68

Social Security, 100, 104

Spending: tips on sound habits, 34-35, 77

Stock market, 120-121

Stocks: records of, 141-142

Student loans: Sallie Mae options, 79-80

T

Tax Reform Act of 1986, 27

Taxes: deductions, 93-94; estate, 137; on mutual funds, 126-127

U

Uniform Gifts to Minors Act, 28

United States Government Series EE Bonds, 28

V

Values, 10-11

W

Wills, 135-138